THE
BIBLE
BRIEF

THE
BIBLE
BRIEF

A Concise and Powerful Guide
for Understanding God's Word

BARBOUR
PUBLISHING

Published by Barbour Publishing, Inc., P.O. Box 719, Uhrichsville,
Ohio 44683, www.barbourbooks.com

Our mission is to publish and distribute inspirational products offering
exceptional value and biblical encouragement to the masses.

 Member of the
Evangelical Christian
Publishers Association

Printed in the United States of America.

Contents

Introduction

This book provides clear, easy-to-understand information about the Bible—text highlights from each of the sixty-six books, vital "nutshell" truths for everyday living, concise descriptions of the most important people, places, and things in God's Word. But please don't stop with this book!

Don't just read *about* the Bible, read the Bible itself. Don't just know *facts* about scripture—know scripture. Take what you learn in this book and put it into practice in regular Bible reading, study, memorization, and meditation.

The Bible Brief gives you a strong start on your travels by identifying and explaining the most important aspects of scripture. Inside this book, you'll find:

- *The Bible Brief,* highlighting passages from all sixty-six books of God's Word, providing a powerful overview in about an hour's reading time.
- *150 Need-to-Know Bible Facts,* explaining key concepts from scripture, such as "God created everything," "Sin is destructive," and "Only Jesus can save us."
- *199 Bible People, Places, and Things,* spotlighting Aaron to Zacchaeus, Bethany to the Tower of Babel, and Adoption to Worship.

When you want to know what's really important in scripture, turn to *The Bible Brief.* This powerful book will start you on a journey of understanding that can truly change your life.

The
BIBLE BRIEF

Read Highlights of the World's Bestselling Book
in About an Hour

Compiled by Tracy M. Sumner, with editorial assistance by Lauren Schneider.

Genesis

In the beginning God created heaven and earth. God said, Let us make man in our image; male and female. God blessed them and said, Be fruitful, replenish the earth: have dominion over every living thing.

God saw every thing he had made, and it was very good. On the seventh day God rested. God blessed the seventh day and sanctified it.

The LORD put man into the garden of Eden and commanded, Of the tree of the knowledge of good and evil, thou shalt not eat: in the day thou eatest thereof thou shalt die.

Now the serpent said unto the woman, Ye shall not die: your eyes shall be opened, and ye shall be as gods. The woman took the fruit and did eat, and gave also unto her husband.

God said unto the serpent, Thou art cursed. I will put enmity between thee and the woman, between thy seed and her seed. Unto Adam he said, In sweat shalt thou eat bread, till thou return unto the ground; dust thou art, unto dust shalt thou return.

God looked upon the earth, and it was corrupt. God said unto Noah, I will destroy the earth. Make an ark. Of every living thing, two of every sort bring into the ark, to keep them alive. Noah went in, and his sons, his wife, and his sons' wives, because of the flood. All flesh died, fowl, cattle, beast, every creeping thing, and every man.

It came to pass, the waters dried up. God spake unto Noah, Go forth of the ark. Bring with thee every living thing, that they may multiply upon the earth. I set my bow in the cloud, a token of a covenant between me and the earth. I will remember my covenant, and waters shall no more become a flood to destroy all flesh.

Shem, Ham, and Japheth: these are the sons of Noah: by these were the nations divided after the flood.

The whole earth was of one language. They said one to another, Let us build a city and a tower, whose top may reach unto heaven; let us make a name, lest we be scattered upon the earth.

The LORD said, Now nothing will be restrained from them which they have imagined. Let us go down and confound their language. Therefore is the name of it Babel; because the LORD did confound the language of all the earth: and from thence did the LORD scatter them.

Terah begat Abram in Ur of the Chaldees. The LORD said unto Abram, Get out of thy country, from thy kindred, unto a land I will shew thee: I will make of thee a great nation; thou shalt be a blessing: I will bless them that bless thee and curse him that curseth thee. So Abram departed and took Sarai his wife. Abram dwelled in the land of Canaan.

The word of the LORD came unto Abram, saying, Fear not: I am thy shield, thy exceeding great reward.

Abram said, God, what wilt thou give me, seeing I go childless?

The word of the LORD came, saying, He that shall come forth out of thine own bowels shall be thine heir. Look toward heaven, and tell the stars, if thou be able to number them: so shall thy seed be.

He believed the LORD; and he counted it to him for righteousness.

The LORD did unto Sarah as he had spoken. Sarah bare Abraham a son in his old age, at the set time of which God had spoken to him. Abraham called the name of his son Isaac.

Isaac was forty years old when he took Rebekah to wife. Isaac intreated the LORD for his wife, because she was barren: and Rebekah conceived. When her days to be delivered were fulfilled, behold, there were twins in her womb. The first came out red; they called his name Esau. After that came his brother out, and his hand took hold on Esau's heel; his name was called Jacob.

Jacob served seven years for Rachel; they seemed unto him but a few days for the love he had to her. Jacob said unto Laban, Give me my wife, for my days are fulfilled.

God remembered Rachel and opened her womb. She bare a son and called his name Joseph.

It came to pass, when Joseph was come unto his brethren, that they stript Joseph out of his coat and cast him into a pit. They sat down to eat bread: they looked, and, behold, a company of Ishmeelites came from Gilead with camels bearing spicery and balm and myrrh, going down to Egypt.

Judah said unto his brethren, What profit is it if we slay our brother and conceal his blood? Let us sell him to the Ishmeelites, and let not our hand be upon him; for he is our brother. And his brethren were content. They drew Joseph out of the pit and sold Joseph to the Ishmeelites for twenty pieces of silver: and they brought Joseph into Egypt.

The LORD was with Joseph, and he was prosperous. At the end of two years, Pharaoh dreamed. Pharaoh said unto Joseph, I have a dream, and I have heard that thou canst interpret it. Joseph said, God hath shewed Pharaoh what he is about to do: there come seven years of great plenty, and after them seven years of famine. Pharaoh said, there is none so wise as thou: See, I have set thee over all the land of Egypt.

When Jacob saw there was corn in Egypt, Jacob said unto his sons, Behold, I have heard there is corn in Egypt: for us from thence; that we may live. And Joseph's ten brethren went down to buy corn in Egypt.

Joseph said unto his brethren, Fear not: am I in the place of God? Ye thought evil against me; but God meant it unto good, to save much people. I will nourish you and your little ones. He comforted them and spake kindly unto them.

Joseph dwelt in Egypt, he and his father's house: and lived an hundred and ten years.

Exodus

The king of Egypt died: and the children of Israel sighed by reason of bondage. God heard their groaning and remembered his covenant with Abraham, Isaac, and Jacob.

Now Moses kept the flock of Jethro his father-in-law: he led the flock to the backside of the desert and came to the mountain of God, Horeb. The angel of the LORD appeared in a flame of fire out of the midst of a bush: and, behold, the bush burned with fire and was not consumed. Moses said, I will turn aside and see this great sight, why the bush is not burnt.

God called unto him out of the bush and said, Moses.

He said, Here am I.

And he said, Draw not nigh: put off thy shoes from thy feet, for the place whereon thou stand is holy ground. I have surely seen the affliction of my people in Egypt and have heard their cry by reason of their taskmasters. I know their sorrows; I am come down to deliver them out of the hand of the Egyptians and to bring them out of that land unto a land flowing with milk and honey. Certainly I will be with thee; and this shall be a token that I have sent thee: When thou hast brought forth the people out of Egypt, ye shall serve God upon this mountain.

Afterward Moses and Aaron went in and told Pharaoh, Thus saith the LORD God of Israel, Let my people go, that they may hold a feast unto me in the wilderness.

Pharaoh said, Who is the LORD, that I should obey his voice to let Israel go? I know not the LORD, neither will I let Israel go.

Moses returned unto the LORD and said, Wherefore hast thou so evil entreated this people? why is it that thou hast sent me? For since I came to Pharaoh to speak in thy name, he hath done evil to this people; neither hast thou delivered thy people at all.

The LORD said, Now shalt thou see what I will do to Pharaoh: for with a strong hand shall he let them go and drive them out of his land. I will harden Pharaoh's heart and multiply my signs and wonders in Egypt. But Pharaoh shall not hearken unto you, that I may lay my hand upon Egypt and bring forth my people the children of Israel out of Egypt by great judgments.

Moses called for all the elders of Israel and said, Take a lamb according to your families, and kill the passover. Take a bunch of hyssop, dip it in the blood, and strike the lintel and two side posts; none of you shall go out the door of his house until morning. For the LORD will pass through to smite the Egyptians; when he seeth the blood upon the lintel, the LORD will pass over the door and not suffer the destroyer to smite you.

It came to pass that at midnight the LORD smote all the firstborn in Egypt, from the firstborn of Pharaoh on his throne unto the firstborn of the captive in the dungeon; and all the firstborn of cattle. Pharaoh rose up in the night, he and his servants and all the Egyptians; there was a great cry in Egypt; for there was not a house where there was not one dead. He called for Moses and Aaron by night and said, Get forth from among my people, both ye and the children of Israel; go, serve the LORD, as ye have said. Also take your flocks and herds, and be gone; and bless me also.

Thus did all the children of Israel; as the LORD commanded Moses and Aaron, so did they. It came to pass the selfsame day that the LORD did bring the children of Israel out of Egypt.

The LORD came down upon mount Sinai: and called Moses. God spake, saying, Thou shalt have no other gods before me. Thou shalt not make any graven image. Thou shalt not take the name of the LORD thy God in vain. Remember the sabbath day, to keep it holy. Honour thy father and thy mother. Thou shalt not kill. Thou shalt not commit adultery. Thou shalt not steal. Thou shalt not bear false witness. Thou shalt not covet any thing that is thy neighbour's.

Leviticus

Walk in my statutes and keep my commandments; then I will give you rain in due season, and the land shall yield her increase and the trees their fruit. Your threshing shall reach unto the vintage, and the vintage shall reach unto the sowing time: ye shall eat your bread to the full and dwell in your land safely. I will give peace in the land, and ye shall lie down, and none shall make you afraid: I will rid evil beasts out of the land, neither shall the sword go through your land. Ye shall chase your enemies, and they shall fall before you by the sword. Five of you shall chase an hundred, and an hundred of you shall put ten thousand to flight.

I will have respect unto you, multiply you, and establish my covenant with you. I set my tabernacle among you: my soul shall not abhor you. I will walk among you and be your God, and ye shall be my people. I am the LORD your God, which brought you out of Egypt, that ye should not be their bondmen; I have broken the bands of your yoke and made you go upright.

But if ye will not hearken unto me and do all these commandments; if ye shall despise my statutes, or if your soul abhor my judgments so that ye break my covenant: I will do this unto you; I will appoint over you terror, consumption, and the burning ague that shall consume the eyes and cause sorrow of heart: and ye shall sow your seed in vain, for your enemies shall eat it. I will set my face against you, and ye shall be slain before your enemies: they that hate you shall reign over you; and ye shall flee when none pursueth you.

And if ye will not yet for all this hearken unto me, I will punish you seven times more for your sins. I will break the pride of your power; I will make your heaven as iron and your earth as brass: your strength shall be spent in vain: for your land shall not yield her increase, neither shall the trees yield their fruits.

Numbers

The LORD spake to Moses in the wilderness of Sinai, in the tabernacle of the congregation, on the first day of the second month in the second year after they were come out of Egypt, saying, Take the sum of all the congregation of the children of Israel, after their families, by the house of their fathers, with the number of their names, every male by their polls; from twenty years old and upward, all that are able to go forth to war in Israel: thou and Aaron shall number them by their armies.

It came to pass on the twentieth day of the second month in the second year that the cloud was taken up from the tabernacle of the testimony. The children of Israel took their journeys out of the wilderness of Sinai; and the cloud rested in the wilderness of Paran.

The LORD spake unto Moses, saying, Send thou men, that they may search the land of Canaan, which I give unto the children of Israel: of every tribe of their fathers shall ye send a man, every one a ruler among them.

Moses sent them to spy out the land of Canaan and said, Get this way southward, and go up into the mountain: see the land, what it is, and the people that dwelleth therein, whether they be strong or weak, few or many.

They returned from searching the land after forty days. They came to Moses, Aaron, and all the congregation of the children of Israel, unto the wilderness of Paran, and brought back word unto them and shewed them the fruit of the land. They said, We came unto the land whither thou sentest us, and surely it floweth with milk and honey; this is the fruit of it. Nevertheless the people be strong that dwell in the land, and the cities are walled and very great.

Caleb stilled the people before Moses and said, Let us go up at once and possess it; for we are well able to overcome it.

But the men that went up with him said, We be not able to go up against the people; for they are stronger than we.

All the children of Israel murmured against Moses and Aaron: the whole congregation said to them, Would God that we had died in Egypt! or in this wilderness! Hath the LORD brought us unto this land to fall by the sword, that our wives and children should be prey? were it not better for us to return into Egypt? They said one to another, Let us make a captain and return into Egypt.

The LORD said to Moses, How long will this people provoke me? how long will it be ere they believe me, for all the signs I have shewed among them? I will smite them with the pestilence and disinherit them, and will make of thee a greater nation and mightier than they.

Moses said, Then the Egyptians shall hear it and tell the inhabitants of this land: for they have heard that thou art among this people, that thy cloud standeth over them, and that thou goest before them by day in a pillar of cloud, and in a pillar of fire by night.

I beseech thee, let the power of my lord be great, as thou hast spoken, saying, The LORD is longsuffering and of great mercy, forgiving iniquity and transgression. Pardon, I beseech thee, the iniquity of this people according unto the greatness of thy mercy.

The LORD said, I have pardoned according to thy word: but as truly as I live, all the earth shall be filled with the glory of the LORD. Because all those men have seen my glory and my miracles, which I did in Egypt and the wilderness, and tempted me now these ten times and not hearkened to my voice; surely they shall not see the land I sware unto their fathers, neither shall any of them that provoked me see it: but my servant Caleb, because he had another spirit with him and hath followed me fully, him will I bring into the land whereinto he went.

Deuteronomy

In the fortieth year, in the eleventh month, on the first day of the month, Moses spake unto the children of Israel according unto all the LORD had given him in commandment unto them. On this side Jordan, in the land of Moab, began Moses to declare this law.

Take heed to thyself, and keep thy soul diligently, lest thou forget the things thine eyes have seen, lest they depart from thy heart all the days of thy life: but teach them thy sons and thy sons'

sons; specially the day thou stoodest before the LORD thy God in Horeb, when the LORD said unto me, Gather the people together, and I will make them hear my words, that they may learn to fear me all the days they live upon the earth, and that they may teach their children.

Take heed unto yourselves, lest ye forget the covenant of the LORD your God, which he made with you, and make a graven image or the likeness of any thing, which the LORD hath forbidden thee. Remember thou wast a servant in the land of Egypt, and the LORD brought thee out thence through a mighty hand and stretched out arm: therefore the LORD commanded thee to keep the sabbath day.

Thou shalt remember the way the LORD led thee these forty years in the wilderness, to humble thee, to prove thee, to know what was in thine heart, whether thou wouldest keep his commandments.

He suffered thee to hunger and fed thee with manna, which thou knewest not, neither did thy fathers know; that he might make thee know that man doth not live by bread only, but by every word that proceedeth out of the mouth of the LORD.

Thy raiment waxed not old upon thee, neither did thy foot swell these forty years. Thou shalt also consider in thine heart that as a man chasteneth his son, so the LORD thy God chasteneth thee. Therefore thou shalt keep the commandments of the LORD, to walk in his ways and to fear him.

Forget not how thou provokedst the LORD to wrath in the wilderness: from the day thou didst depart out of Egypt until ye came unto this place, ye have been rebellious against the LORD.

Moses the servant of the LORD died there in the land of Moab, according to the word of the LORD. And he buried him in a valley in the land of Moab.

Moses was an hundred and twenty years old when he died. And Joshua son of Nun was full of the spirit of wisdom; for Moses had laid his hands upon him: the children of Israel hearkened unto him and did as the LORD commanded Moses.

Joshua

After the death of Moses, the LORD spake unto Joshua, Moses' minister, saying, Moses my servant is dead; therefore arise, go over Jordan, and all this people, unto the land I give to them.

Every place the sole of your foot shall tread upon, that have I given unto you, as I said unto Moses. There shall not any man be able to stand before thee all the days of thy life: as I was with Moses, so I will be with thee: I will not fail thee nor forsake thee.

Then Joshua commanded the officers of the people, saying, Pass through the host and command the people, Prepare victuals; for within three days ye shall pass over Jordan to go in to possess the land the LORD giveth you.

To the Reubenites, the Gadites, and half the tribe of Manasseh spake Joshua, saying, Remember the word Moses commanded you, saying, The LORD your God hath given you rest and hath given you this land.

They answered Joshua, All that thou commandest us we will do, and whithersoever thou sendest us, we will go.

A long time after the LORD had given rest unto Israel from all their enemies round about, Joshua waxed old. Joshua called for all Israel and for their elders, heads, judges, and officers and said unto them, I am stricken in age: ye have seen all that the LORD hath done unto all these nations because of you; for the LORD your God hath fought for you.

Behold, I have divided unto you by lot these nations that remain, to be an inheritance for your tribes, from Jordan, with all the nations I have cut off, even unto the great sea westward.

Judges

When Joshua had let the people go, the children of Israel went every man unto his inheritance to possess the land. The people served the LORD all the days of Joshua and all the days of the elders that outlived Joshua. And Joshua died, being an hundred and ten years old. All that generation were gathered unto their fathers: and there arose another generation after them, which knew not the LORD, nor yet the works he had done for Israel.

The children of Israel did evil in the sight of the LORD and served Baalim: they forsook the God of their fathers. The anger of the LORD was hot against Israel, and he delivered them into the hands of their enemies round about.

Nevertheless the LORD raised up judges, which delivered them out of the hand of those that spoiled them. Yet they would not hearken unto their judges, but went after other gods and bowed themselves to them: they turned quickly out of the way their fathers walked in.

The children of Israel did evil: and the LORD delivered them into the hand of Midian seven years. Israel was greatly impoverished because of the Midianites; and the children of Israel cried to the LORD. There came an angel of the LORD and sat under an oak in Ophrah, that pertained unto Joash the Abiezrite: his son Gideon threshed wheat by the winepress to hide it from the Midianites. The angel of the LORD appeared unto him and said, The LORD is with thee, mighty man of valour.

Gideon said, Oh my Lord, if the LORD be with us, why then is all this befallen us? and where be all his miracles which our fathers told us of, saying, Did not the LORD bring us up from Egypt? but now the LORD hath forsaken us and delivered us into the hands of the Midianites.

The LORD looked upon him and said, Go in this thy might, and thou shalt save Israel from the hand of the Midianites: have not I sent thee?

It came to pass, as soon as Gideon was dead, the children of Israel turned again, and went a whoring after Baalim. In those days there was no king in Israel: every man did that which was right in his own eyes.

Ruth

When the judges ruled, there was a famine. A man went to Moab, he, his wife, and two sons. Elimelech died; Mahlon and Chilion died also.

Naomi said unto her daughters-in-law, Go, return each to her mother's house.

Ruth said, Intreat me not to leave: whither thou goest, I will go; thy people shall be my people, thy God my God.

So Naomi returned, and Ruth the Moabitess with her, to Bethlehem in the beginning of harvest. Naomi had a kinsman of wealth; his name was Boaz.

Ruth said, Let me go to the field and glean.

Boaz commanded his men, saying, Let her glean even among the sheaves, reproach her not.

Naomi said, Blessed be he of the LORD, who hath not left off his kindness. The man is one of our next kinsmen.

Boaz said, I do the part of a kinsman to thee. So Boaz took Ruth, and she was his wife: and she bare a son. They called his name Obed: he is the father of Jesse, the father of David.

1 Samuel

All Israel from Dan to Beersheba knew Samuel was established to be a prophet of the LORD. The LORD appeared again in Shiloh: for the LORD revealed himself to Samuel in Shiloh by the word of the LORD.

All the elders of Israel gathered together and came to Samuel and said, Behold, thou art old, and thy sons walk not in thy ways: now make us a king to judge us like all the nations.

But the thing displeased Samuel, when they said, Give us a king. Samuel prayed unto the LORD. And the LORD said unto Samuel, Hearken unto the voice of the people: for they have not rejected thee but have rejected me, that I should not reign over them.

Now the LORD had told Samuel a day before Saul came, Tomorrow about this time I will send a man out of the land of Benjamin, and thou shalt anoint him to be captain over my people Israel, that he may save my people out of the hand of the Philistines: for I have looked upon my people, because their cry is come unto me. When Samuel saw Saul, the LORD said, Behold the man I spake to thee of!

When he had reigned two years over Israel, Saul chose three thousand men of Israel; two thousand were with Saul in Michmash and in mount Bethel, and a thousand were with Jonathan in Gibeah: the rest of the people he sent every man to his tent.

Jonathan smote the garrison of the Philistines in Geba, and the Philistines heard of it. Saul blew the trumpet throughout all the land, saying, Let the Hebrews hear.

Saul said, Bring hither a burnt offering to me, and peace offerings. As soon as he had made an end of offering the burnt offering, Samuel came and said, What hast thou done?

Saul said, Because I saw that the people were scattered from me, and that thou camest not within the days appointed, and that the Philistines gathered at Michmash; therefore said I, The Philistines will come down now upon me to Gilgal, and I have not made supplication unto the LORD: I forced myself therefore and offered a burnt offering.

Samuel said to Saul, Thou hast done foolishly: thou hast not kept the commandment of the LORD thy God: for now would the LORD have established thy kingdom upon Israel for ever. But now thy kingdom shall not continue: the LORD hath sought a man after his own heart and commanded him to be captain over his people, because thou hast not kept that which the LORD commanded thee.

The LORD said unto Samuel, How long wilt thou mourn for Saul, seeing I have rejected him from reigning over Israel? fill thine horn with oil, and go, I will send thee to Jesse the Bethlehemite: for I have provided me a king among his sons.

Samuel took the horn of oil and anointed him in the midst of his brethren: and the Spirit of the LORD came upon David from that day forward.

2 Samuel

It came to pass that David enquired of the LORD, Shall I go up into any of the cities of Judah?

The LORD said unto him, Go up.

David said, Whither shall I go up?

And he said, Unto Hebron.

Then came all the tribes of Israel to David unto Hebron, saying, Behold, we are thy bone and thy flesh. In time past, when Saul was king over us, thou leddest out and broughtest in Israel: and the LORD said to thee, Thou shalt feed my people Israel and be a captain over Israel. So all the elders of Israel came to Hebron; and David made a league with them before the LORD: and they anointed David king over Israel.

After the year was expired, at the time when kings go forth to battle, David sent Joab, his servants, and all Israel; they destroyed the children of Ammon and besieged Rabbah. But David tarried at Jerusalem.

In an eveningtide David arose from his bed and walked upon the roof of the king's house: from the roof he saw a woman washing herself; and the woman was very beautiful. David enquired after the woman. And one said, Is not this Bathsheba, wife of Uriah the Hittite?

David sent messengers and took her; she came in unto him, and he lay with her: and she returned to her house. The woman conceived and sent and told David, I am with child.

David wrote a letter to Joab, saying, Set Uriah in the forefront of the hottest battle, and retire from him, that he may die. And there fell some of the servants of David; and Uriah the Hittite died also. When the wife of Uriah heard that her husband was dead, she mourned. When the mourning was past, David fetched her to his house, and she became his wife and bare him a son. But the thing David had done displeased the LORD.

David said unto Nathan, I have sinned against the LORD.

Nathan said, The LORD hath put away thy sin; thou shalt not die. Howbeit, because by this deed thou hast given great occasion to the enemies of the LORD to blaspheme, the child born unto thee shall surely die.

David said unto his servants, Is the child dead? They said, He is. David comforted Bathsheba, and went and lay with her: she bare a son, and called his name Solomon: and the LORD loved him.

1 Kings

The days of David drew nigh that he should die; he charged Solomon his son, saying, I go the way of all the earth: be strong therefore, and shew thyself a man; keep the charge of the LORD thy God, to walk in his ways, to keep his statutes, commandments, judgments, and testimonies, as it is written in the law of Moses, that thou mayest prosper in all thou doest.

So David slept with his fathers and was buried in the city of David. The days that David reigned over Israel were forty years: seven years reigned he in Hebron, thirty-three years in Jerusalem. Then sat Solomon upon the throne of David; and his kingdom was established greatly.

Solomon loved the LORD, walking in the statutes of David his father: only he sacrificed and burnt incense in high places. The king went to Gibeon to sacrifice there. In Gibeon the LORD appeared to Solomon in a dream and said, Ask what I shall give thee.

Solomon said, Give thy servant an understanding heart to judge thy people, that I may discern between good and bad.

God said, Because thou hast not asked for long life; neither riches for thyself, nor the life of thine enemies; but for thyself understanding to discern judgment; behold, I have done according to thy words: I have given thee a wise and understanding heart.

It came to pass in the four hundred eightieth year after the children of Israel were come out of Egypt, in the fourth year of Solomon's reign over Israel, that he began to build the house of the LORD.

When Solomon was old, his wives turned away his heart after other gods: and his heart was not perfect with the LORD, as was the heart of David his father. Solomon did evil and went not fully after the LORD.

The time that Solomon reigned in Jerusalem over all Israel was forty years. Solomon slept with his fathers and was buried in the city of David: Rehoboam his son reigned in his stead.

The king answered the people roughly, saying, My father made your yoke heavy, and I will add to your yoke: my father chastised you with whips, I will chastise you with scorpions. When all Israel saw that the king hearkened not unto them, the people answered, saying, What portion have we in David? So Israel departed unto their tents. But as for the children of Israel in the cities of Judah, Rehoboam reigned over them.

2 Kings

In the twelfth year of Ahaz king of Judah began Hoshea to reign in Samaria over Israel nine years. He did evil in the sight of the LORD, but not as the kings of Israel before him. Against him came up Shalmaneser king of Assyria. The king of Assyria came throughout all the land and went up to Samaria and besieged it three years. In the ninth year of Hoshea the king of Assyria took Samaria, carried Israel away into Assyria, and placed them in the cities of the Medes.

For the children of Israel had sinned against the LORD, which had brought them up out of Egypt, from under the hand of Pharaoh, and had feared other gods and walked in the statutes of the heathen, whom the LORD cast out from before the children of Israel, and of the kings of Israel, which they had made.

Josiah was eight years old when he began to reign, and he reigned thirty-one years in Jerusalem. He did that which was right in the sight of the LORD, walked in all the way of David his father, and turned not aside to the right or to the left.

The king sent, and they gathered unto him all the elders of Judah and Jerusalem. The king went up into the house of the LORD, and all the men of Judah and all the inhabitants of Jerusalem with him, the priests, prophets, and all the people, both small and great: he read in their ears all the words of the book of the covenant which was found in the house of the LORD.

The king stood by a pillar and made a covenant before the

LORD, to walk after the LORD and to keep his commandments with all their heart and soul, to perform the words of this covenant that were written in this book. And all the people stood to the covenant.

Notwithstanding the LORD turned not from the fierceness of his great wrath, wherewith his anger was kindled against Judah, because of all the provocations that had provoked him withal. The LORD said, I will remove Judah also out of my sight, as I have removed Israel, and will cast off this city Jerusalem which I have chosen, and the house of which I said, My name shall be there.

Jehoiachin was eighteen years old when he began to reign, and he reigned in Jerusalem three months. He did evil in the sight of the LORD, according to all his father had done.

At that time Nebuchadnezzar king of Babylon came against the city, and his servants did besiege it.

In the fifth month, on the seventh day of the month, which is the nineteenth year of Nebuchadnezzar king of Babylon, came Nebuzaradan, captain of the guard, a servant of the king of Babylon, unto Jerusalem: he burnt the house of the LORD, and the king's house, and all the houses of Jerusalem, and every great man's house burnt he with fire. So Judah was carried away out of their land.

1 Chronicles

David the king said unto all the congregation, Solomon my son, whom alone God hath chosen, is yet young and tender, and the work is great: for the palace is not for man but for the LORD.

Now I have prepared with all my might for the house of my God the gold for things to be made of gold, the silver for things of silver, the brass for things of brass, the iron for things of iron, and wood for things of wood; onyx stones, stones to be set, glistering stones, and of divers colours, all manner of precious stones, and marble stones in abundance.

Moreover, because I have set my affection to the house of my God, I have of mine own gold and silver given to the house of my God over and above all I have prepared for the holy house. Who then is willing to consecrate his service this day unto the LORD?

Then the chief of the fathers and princes of the tribes of Israel and the captains of thousands and of hundreds, with the rulers of the king's work, offered willingly for the service of the house of God of gold five thousand talents and ten thousand drams, and of silver ten thousand talents, and of brass eighteen thousand talents, and one hundred thousand talents of iron.

Wherefore David blessed the LORD before all the congregation: David said, Blessed be thou, LORD God of Israel our father, for ever and ever. Thine is the greatness, the power, the glory, the victory, and the majesty: for all that is in heaven and in earth is thine; thine is the kingdom, and thou art exalted as head above all. Both riches and honour come of thee, and thou reignest over all; in thine hand is power and might; in thine hand it is to make great and to give strength unto all. Therefore we thank thee and praise thy glorious name.

2 Chronicles

Asa did that which was good and right in the eyes of the LORD his God: he took away the altars of the strange gods and the high places, brake down the images, and cut down the groves: and commanded Judah to seek the God of their fathers and to do the law and the commandment.

The Spirit of God came upon Azariah son of Oded: he went out to meet Asa and said, Hear me, Asa, and all Judah and Benjamin; the LORD is with you while ye be with him; if ye seek him, he will be found of you; but if ye forsake him, he will forsake you. Now for a long season Israel hath been without the true God, without a teaching priest, and without law. But when they in their trouble did turn unto the God of Israel and sought him, he was found of them. In those times there was no peace to him that went out, nor to him that came in, but great vexations were upon all the inhabitants of the countries. And nation was destroyed of nation, and city of city: for God did vex them with all adversity. Be strong therefore, and let not your hands be weak: for your work shall be rewarded.

The God of their fathers sent to them by his messengers, because he had compassion on his people and his dwelling place: but they mocked the messengers of God, despised his words, and misused his prophets, until the wrath of the LORD arose against his people, till there was no remedy. Therefore he brought upon them the king of the Chaldees, who slew their young men with the sword in the house of their sanctuary and had no compassion upon young man or maiden, old man, or him that stooped for age: he gave them all into his hand. All the vessels of the house of God, great and small, and the treasures of the house of the LORD, and the treasures of the king and of his princes; all these he brought to Babylon. They burnt the house of God, brake down the wall of Jerusalem, burnt all the palaces thereof with fire, and destroyed all the goodly vessels thereof. Them that had escaped from the sword carried he away to Babylon; where they were servants to him and his sons until the reign of the kingdom of Persia: to fulfill the word of the LORD by the mouth of Jeremiah, until the land had enjoyed her sabbaths: for as long as she lay desolate she kept sabbath, to fulfill threescore and ten years.

Now in the first year of Cyrus king of Persia, that the word of the LORD spoken by Jeremiah might be accomplished, the LORD stirred the spirit of Cyrus, that he made a proclamation in writing, saying, Thus saith Cyrus, All the kingdoms of the earth hath the God of heaven given me; and he hath charged me to build him an house in Jerusalem. Who is there among you of all his people? The LORD his God be with him, and let him go.

Ezra

Then rose up the chief of the fathers of Judah and Benjamin, and the priests, and the Levites, with all them whose spirit God had raised, to go up to build the house of the LORD.

After these things, in the reign of Artaxerxes king of Persia, Ezra son of Seraiah went up from Babylon; he was a scribe in the law of Moses, which the God of Israel had given: and the king granted his request, according to the hand of the LORD his God upon him.

For Ezra had prepared his heart to seek the law of the LORD and to do it, and to teach in Israel statutes and judgments.

Nehemiah

The words of Nehemiah. It came to pass that Hanani, one of my brethren, came, he and certain men of Judah; and I asked them concerning the Jews which were left of the captivity, and concerning Jerusalem.

They said unto me, The remnant that are left there in the province are in great affliction: the wall of Jerusalem is broken down, and the gates thereof are burned.

When I heard these words, I sat down and wept, mourned certain days, fasted, prayed before the God of heaven, and said, I beseech thee, LORD God: let thine ear be attentive, that thou may hear the prayer of thy servant.

I was the king's cupbearer. I said unto the king, If thy servant have found favour in thy sight, send me unto Judah, that I may build it. It pleased the king to send me.

When the wall was built, and I had set up the doors, I gave my brother Hanani charge over Jerusalem: for he was a faithful man, and feared God above many.

Esther

King Ahasuerus made a feast unto all the people in Shushan. On the seventh day, when the heart of the king was merry with wine, he commanded the chamberlains to bring Vashti the queen before the king to show the people her beauty. But Vashti refused to come: therefore anger burned in the king. The king said to the wise men, What shall we do unto the queen?

Memucan answered, Let it be written that Vashti come no more before king Ahasuerus; and let the king give her royal estate unto another better than she.

Then said the king's servants, Let there be fair young virgins sought for the king: and let the maiden which pleaseth the king be queen instead of Vashti.

Now in Shushan there was a certain Jew, Mordecai. He brought up Hadassah, that is, Esther, his uncle's daughter: the maid was beautiful.

Esther was brought unto the king's house. Esther obtained favour in the sight of all that looked upon her. So Esther was taken unto Ahasuerus. The king loved Esther above all the women and made her queen. Esther had not yet shewed her kindred nor her people; as Mordecai had charged her.

After these things did Ahasuerus promote Haman. Haman sought to destroy all Jews throughout the kingdom. Haman said unto Ahasuerus, There is a certain people dispersed among the people in thy kingdom; their laws are diverse from all people; neither keep they the king's laws. Let it be written that they may be destroyed.

The king said, Do with them as seemeth good to thee.

When Mordecai perceived all that was done, Mordecai rent his clothes.

Then called Esther for Hatach, one of the chamberlains, and gave him a commandment to Mordecai, to know what it was and why it was.

Mordecai gave him the copy of the decree, to shew it unto Esther and to charge her that she should go in unto the king to make request for her people.

Hatach told Esther the words of Mordecai. Esther gave him commandment unto Mordecai; Whosoever shall come unto the king, who is not called, there is one law to put him to death, except such to whom the king shall hold out the golden sceptre: but I have not been called to come in thirty days.

Mordecai commanded to answer Esther, If thou holdest thy peace at this time, then shall there deliverance arise to the Jews from another place; but thou and thy father's house shall be destroyed: and who knoweth whether thou art come to the kingdom for such a time as this?

Esther bade them return this answer, Gather all the Jews in Shushan, and fast for me three days: I also will fast; and so will I go in unto the king: and if I perish, I perish.

On the third day, Esther stood in the inner court of the king's house. The king saw Esther and held out the sceptre in his hand. Said the king, What is thy request?

Esther answered, Let the king and Haman come this day unto the banquet I have prepared.

So the king and Haman came to banquet with Esther.

The king said, What is thy petition?

Esther answered, Let my life be given me, and my people. For we are sold to be destroyed.

The king said, Who is he that durst presume in his heart to do so?

Esther said, This wicked Haman.

Harbonah, one of the chamberlains, said before the king, Behold, the gallows, which Haman had made for Mordecai, standeth in the house of Haman.

Then the king said, Hang him thereon.

Esther stood before the king and said, Let it be written to reverse the letters devised by Haman. For how can I endure to see the evil that shall come unto my people?

The king said unto Esther and Mordecai, Write ye also for the Jews, as it liketh you, in the king's name.

The commandment was published unto all people, that the

Jews should be ready against that day to avenge themselves on their enemies.

Mordecai went out from the presence of the king in royal apparel: and the city of Shushan rejoiced. Many people of the land became Jews; for the fear of the Jews fell upon them.

Job

Job was perfect and upright, one that feared God and eschewed evil.

The LORD said unto Satan, Hast thou considered my servant Job, that there is none like him in the earth, a perfect and upright man?

Satan answered, Doth Job fear God for nought? Hast not thou made a hedge about him, his house, and all he hath? thou hast blessed the work of his hands, and his substance is increased in the land. But put forth thine hand now and touch all he hath, and he will curse thee to thy face.

The LORD said unto Satan, Behold, all he hath is in thy power; only upon himself put not forth thine hand. So Satan went forth from the presence of the LORD.

There came a messenger unto Job and said, The oxen were plowing, and the asses feeding beside them: and the Sabeans fell upon them and took them away; yea, they have slain the servants with the sword; I only am escaped to tell thee.

While he was yet speaking, there came another and said, Thy sons and daughters were eating and drinking wine in their eldest brother's house: there came a great wind from the wilderness and smote the house, and it fell upon the young men, and they are dead; I only am escaped to tell thee.

Job arose, rent his mantle, shaved his head, fell down upon the ground, worshipped, and said, Naked came I out of my mother's womb, and naked shall I return thither: the LORD gave, and the LORD hath taken away; blessed be the name of the LORD. In all this Job sinned not, nor charged God foolishly.

The Lord said unto Satan, Hast thou considered Job? still he holdeth fast his integrity.

Satan answered, All a man hath will he give for his life. But touch his flesh, and he will curse thee to thy face.

The Lord said, Behold, he is in thine hand; but save his life.

So went Satan forth from the presence of the LORD and smote Job with boils from the sole of his foot unto his crown. He took a potsherd to scrape himself withal; and he sat down among the ashes.

After this opened Job his mouth and cursed his day. Job said, Let the day perish wherein I was born, and the night in which it was said, There is a man-child conceived. Let that day be darkness; let not God regard it from above, neither let the light shine upon it.

The LORD answered Job, Who is this that darkeneth counsel by words without knowledge? Gird up thy loins like a man; for I will demand of thee, and answer thou me.

Where wast thou when I laid the foundations of the earth? declare, if thou hast understanding. Who hath laid the measures thereof? or who hath stretched the line upon it? Whereupon are the foundations thereof fastened? or who laid the corner stone thereof; when the morning stars sang together, and all the sons of God shouted for joy?

Job answered the LORD, I know thou canst do every thing and no thought can be withholden from thee. Who is he that hideth counsel without knowledge? therefore have I uttered that I understood not; things too wonderful for me, which I knew not.

Hear, I beseech thee, and I will speak: I will demand of thee, and declare thou unto me. I have heard of thee by the hearing of the ear: but now mine eye seeth thee. Wherefore I abhor myself and repent in dust and ashes.

Psalms

Blessed is the man that walketh not in the counsel of the ungodly, nor standeth in the way of sinners, nor sitteth in the seat of the scornful. But his delight is in the law of the LORD; and in his law he meditates day and night. He shall be like a tree planted by rivers of water, that bringeth forth his fruit in his season; his leaf shall not wither; whatsoever he doeth shall prosper.

I will love thee, O LORD, my strength. The LORD is my rock, my fortress, and my deliverer; my God, my strength, in whom I will trust; my buckler, the horn of my salvation, and my high tower. I will call upon the LORD, who is worthy to be praised: so shall I be saved from mine enemies.

The LORD is my shepherd; I shall not want. He maketh me to lie down in green pastures: he leadeth me beside still waters. He restoreth my soul: he leadeth me in paths of righteousness for his name's sake. Yea, though I walk through the valley of the shadow of death, I will fear no evil: for thou art with me; thy rod and thy staff they comfort me. Thou preparest a table before me in the presence of mine enemies: thou anointest my head with oil; my cup runneth over. Surely goodness and mercy shall follow me all the days of my life: and I will dwell in the house of the LORD for ever.

Blessed is he whose transgression is forgiven, whose sin is covered. Blessed is the man unto whom the LORD imputeth not iniquity, and in whose spirit there is no guile. When I kept silence, my bones waxed old through my roaring all the day long. For day and night thy hand was heavy upon me: my moisture is turned into the drought of summer. I acknowledge my sin unto thee, and mine iniquity have I not hid. I said, I will confess my transgressions unto the LORD; and thou forgavest the iniquity of my sin.

Delight thyself in the LORD: and he shall give thee the desires of thine heart. Commit thy way unto the LORD; trust also in him; and he shall bring it to pass. He shall bring forth thy righteousness as the light, and thy judgment as the noonday.

As the hart panteth after the water brooks, so panteth my soul after thee, O God. My soul thirsteth for the living God: when shall I come and appear before God? My tears have been my meat day and night, while they continually say unto me, Where is thy God? When I remember these things, I pour out my soul in me: for I had gone with the multitude, I went with them to the house of God, with the voice of joy and praise, with a multitude that kept holyday.

Blessed are the undefiled in the way, who walk in the law of the LORD. Blessed are they that keep his testimonies and seek him with the whole heart. They also do no iniquity: they walk in his ways. Thou hast commanded us to keep thy precepts diligently. O that my ways were directed to keep thy statutes! Then shall I not be ashamed, when I have respect unto all thy commandments. I will praise thee with uprightness of heart, when I shall have learned thy righteous judgments. I will keep thy statutes.

Wherewithal shall a young man cleanse his way? by taking heed thereto according to thy word. With my whole heart have I sought thee: let me not wander from thy commandments. Thy word have I hid in mine heart, that I might not sin against thee.

Proverbs

The proverbs of Solomon, son of David, king of Israel; to know wisdom and instruction; to perceive the words of understanding; to receive the instruction of wisdom, justice, judgment, and equity; to give subtilty to the simple, to the young man knowledge and discretion.

The fear of the LORD is the beginning of knowledge: but fools despise wisdom and instruction.

My son, if thou wilt receive my words and hide my commandments; so that thou incline thine ear unto wisdom and apply thine heart to understanding; yea, if thou criest after knowledge and liftest up thy voice for understanding; if thou seekest her as silver and searchest for her as for hid treasures; then shalt thou understand the fear of the LORD and find the knowledge of God. For the LORD giveth wisdom: out of his mouth cometh knowledge and understanding. Trust in the LORD with all thine heart; lean not unto thine own understanding. In all thy ways acknowledge him, and he shall direct thy paths. Be not wise in thine own eyes: fear the LORD, and depart from evil.

Keep thy heart with all diligence; for out of it are the issues of life. Put away from thee a froward mouth and perverse lips.

A soft answer turneth away wrath: but grievous words stir up anger. The tongue of the wise useth knowledge aright: but the mouth of fools poureth out foolishness. A wholesome tongue is a tree of life: but perverseness therein is a breach in the spirit.

Who can find a virtuous woman? for her price is far above rubies. The heart of her husband doth safely trust in her so that he shall have no need of spoil. She will do him good and not evil all the days of her life.

Favour is deceitful, and beauty is vain: but a woman that feareth the LORD shall be praised. Give her of the fruit of her hands; and let her own works praise her in the gates.

Ecclesiates

The words of the Preacher, son of David, king in Jerusalem.

Vanity of vanities, saith the Preacher, all is vanity. What profit hath a man of all his labour which he taketh under the sun?

I said in mine heart, I will prove thee with mirth, therefore enjoy pleasure: and, behold, this also is vanity. I said of laughter, It is mad: and of mirth, What doeth it?

Let us hear the conclusion of the whole matter: Fear God and keep his commandments: for this is the whole duty of man. God shall bring every work into judgment, with every secret thing, whether it be good or evil.

Song of Solomon

The song of songs, which is Solomon's.

Let him kiss me with the kisses of his mouth: for thy love is better than wine.

I am the rose of Sharon and the lily of the valleys. As the lily among thorns, so is my love among the daughters. As the apple tree among the trees of the wood, so is my beloved among the sons.

He brought me to the banqueting house, and his banner over me was love.

Isaiah

The vision of Isaiah, son of Amoz, which he saw concerning Judah and Jerusalem in the days of Uzziah, Jotham, Ahaz, and Hezekiah, kings of Judah.

Hear, O heavens, and give ear, O earth: for the LORD hath spoken, I have nourished and brought up children, and they have rebelled against me.

Woe unto them that draw iniquity with cords of vanity, and sin as it were with a cart rope: that say, Let him hasten his work, that we may see it! Woe unto them that call evil good, and good evil; that put darkness for light, and light for darkness; that put bitter for sweet, and sweet for bitter!

Therefore as the fire devoureth the stubble and the flame consumeth the chaff, so their root shall be as rottenness and their blossom shall go up as dust: because they have cast away the law of the LORD and despised the word of the Holy One of Israel. Therefore is the anger of the LORD kindled against his people, and he hath stretched forth his hand against them and smitten them.

In the year that king Uzziah died I saw the LORD sitting upon a throne, high and lifted up, and his train filled the temple. Above it stood the seraphims: one cried unto another and said, Holy, holy,

holy is the LORD of hosts: the whole earth is full of his glory. The posts of the door moved at the voice of him that cried, and the house was filled with smoke.

Then said I, Woe is me! I am undone; because I am a man of unclean lips, and I dwell in the midst of a people of unclean lips: for mine eyes have seen the King.

Then flew one of the seraphims unto me, having a live coal in his hand, which he had taken with tongs from off the altar: he laid it upon my mouth and said, This hath touched thy lips; and thine iniquity is taken away and thy sin purged.

Also I heard the voice of the Lord, saying, Whom shall I send, and who will go for us? Then said I, Here am I; send me.

Hear now, O house of David; Is it a small thing for you to weary men, but will ye weary my God also? Therefore the Lord himself shall give you a sign; behold, a virgin shall conceive and bear a son and shall call his name Immanuel.

For unto us a child is born, a son is given: and the government shall be upon his shoulder: his name shall be called Wonderful, Counsellor, The mighty God, The everlasting Father, The Prince of Peace. Of the increase of his government and peace there shall be no end, upon the throne of David, and upon his kingdom, to order it and to establish it with judgment and justice from henceforth even for ever.

Who hath believed our report? and to whom is the arm of the LORD revealed? For he shall grow up before him as a tender plant and as a root out of dry ground: he hath no form nor comeliness; and when we shall see him, there is no beauty that we should desire him.

He is despised and rejected of men; a man of sorrows and acquainted with grief: we hid our faces from him; he was despised, and we esteemed him not. Surely he hath borne our griefs and carried our sorrows: yet we did esteem him stricken, smitten of God, and afflicted. But he was wounded for our transgressions, he was bruised for our iniquities.

All we like sheep have gone astray; we have turned every one to his own way; and the LORD hath laid on him the iniquity of us all. He was oppressed and afflicted, yet he opened not his mouth: he is brought as a lamb to the slaughter, and as a sheep before her shearers is dumb, so he openeth not his mouth.

Yet it pleased the LORD to bruise him; he hath put him to grief: when thou shalt make his soul an offering for sin, he shall see his seed, he shall prolong his days, and the pleasure of the LORD shall prosper in his hand. He shall see of the travail of his soul and be satisfied: by his knowledge shall my righteous servant justify many; for he shall bear their iniquities.

The Spirit of the Lord GOD is upon me; because the LORD hath anointed me to preach good tidings unto the meek; he hath sent me to bind up the brokenhearted, to proclaim liberty to the captives and the opening of the prison to them that are bound; to proclaim the acceptable year of the LORD and the day of vengeance of our God; to comfort all that mourn.

Jeremiah

The words of Jeremiah, son of Hilkiah, of the priests in Anathoth in the land of Benjamin: The word of the LORD came unto me, saying, Before I formed thee in the belly I knew thee; before thou came out of the womb I sanctified thee and ordained thee a prophet unto the nations.

Then the LORD put forth his hand and touched my mouth. The LORD said unto me, Behold, I have put my words in thy mouth.

The word of the LORD came to me, saying, Go and cry in the ears of Jerusalem, saying, Thus saith the LORD; I remember thee, the kindness of thy youth, the love of thine espousals, when thou wentest after me in the wilderness, in a land that was not sown. Israel was holiness unto the LORD and the firstfruits of his increase: all that devour him shall offend; evil shall come upon them.

Thus saith the LORD, What iniquity have your fathers found

in me, that they are gone far from me and have walked after vanity and are become vain? Neither said they, Where is the LORD that brought us up out of Egypt, that led us through the wilderness, through a land of deserts and pits, through a land of drought and the shadow of death, through a land no man passed through and where no man dwelt?

If thou wilt return, O Israel, saith the LORD, return unto me: and if thou wilt put away thine abominations, then shalt thou not remove. Thou shalt swear, The LORD liveth in truth, in judgment, and in righteousness; the nations shall bless themselves in him, and in him shall they glory.

Thus saith the LORD to the men of Judah and Jerusalem, Break up your fallow ground, and sow not among thorns. Circumcise yourselves to the LORD, and take away the foreskins of your heart: lest my fury come forth like fire and burn that none can quench it, because of the evil of your doings.

How do ye say, We are wise, and the law of the LORD is with us? Certainly in vain made he it; the pen of the scribes is in vain. The wise men are ashamed, they are dismayed and taken: they have rejected the word of the LORD; what wisdom is in them? Therefore will I give their wives unto others and their fields to them that shall inherit them: for every one from the least unto the greatest is given to covetousness, from the prophet even unto the priest every one dealeth falsely.

Thus saith the LORD unto this people, Thus have they loved to wander, they have not refrained their feet, therefore the LORD doth not accept them; he will now remember their iniquity and visit their sins.

Thus saith the LORD, After seventy years be accomplished at Babylon I will visit you and perform my good word toward you, in causing you to return to this place. For I know the thoughts I think toward you, thoughts of peace and not of evil, to give you an expected end. Then shall ye call upon me and pray unto me, and

I will hearken unto you. Ye shall seek me and find me when ye search for me with all your heart. I will be found of you: I will turn away your captivity and gather you from all the nations and all the places whither I have driven you; and I will bring you again into the place whence I caused you to be carried away captive.

Again there shall be heard in this place, which ye say shall be desolate, even in the cities of Judah and in the streets of Jerusalem that are desolate, without man and without beast, the voice of joy and of gladness, the voice of the bridegroom and of the bride, the voice of them that shall say, Praise the LORD of hosts: for the LORD is good; his mercy endureth for ever: and of them that shall bring the sacrifice of praise into the house of the LORD. For I will cause to return the captivity of the land, as at the first, saith the LORD.

Lamentations

How doth the city sit solitary, that was full of people! how is she become as a widow! she that was great among the nations and princess among the provinces, how is she become tributary!
　　She weepeth in the night, and her tears are on her cheeks: among all her lovers she hath none to comfort her: all her friends have dealt treacherously with her, they are become her enemies.

This I recall to my mind, therefore have I hope. It is of the LORD's mercies that we are not consumed, because his compassions fail not. They are new every morning: great is thy faithfulness.

Ezekiel

It came to pass, as I was among the captives by the river Chebar, that the heavens were opened, and I saw visions of God.

In the fifth year of king Jehoiachin's captivity, the word of the LORD came expressly unto Ezekiel the priest, son of Buzi, in the land of the Chaldeans by the river Chebar; and the hand of the LORD was there upon him.

He said unto me, Son of man, I send thee to the children of Israel, to a rebellious nation that hath rebelled against me: they and their fathers have transgressed against me, even unto this very day. For they are impudent children and stiffhearted. I send thee unto them; thou shalt say, Thus saith the Lord GOD. And they, whether they will hear or forbear, yet shall know that there hath been a prophet among them.

Son of man, be not afraid of them, though briers and thorns be with thee and thou dost dwell among scorpions: be not afraid of their words, nor dismayed at their looks, though they be a rebellious house. Thou shalt speak my words unto them, whether they will hear or forbear: for they are most rebellious. But thou, son of man, hear what I say unto thee; Be not rebellious like that rebellious house: open thy mouth, and eat that I give thee.

Again the word of the LORD came unto me, saying, Son of man, speak to the children of thy people and say, When I bring the sword upon a land, if the people of the land take a man of their coasts and set him for their watchman: if when he seeth the sword come upon the land, he blow the trumpet and warn the people; then whosoever heareth the sound of the trumpet and taketh not warning; if the sword come and take him away, his blood shall be upon his own head.

The word of the LORD came unto me, saying, Son of man, prophesy against the shepherds of Israel and say, Woe to the shepherds of Israel that feed themselves! should not the shepherds feed the flocks? Ye eat the fat, ye clothe you with the wool, ye kill them that are fed: but ye feed not the flock.

Also prophesy unto the mountains of Israel and say, Ye mountains of Israel, hear the word of the LORD: Because the enemy hath said against you, Aha, even the ancient high places are ours in possession; because they have made you desolate and swallowed you up on every side, that ye might be a possession unto the residue of the heathen, and ye are taken up in the lips of talkers and are an infamy of the people: therefore hear the word of the Lord GOD; Thus saith the Lord GOD to the mountains, the hills, the rivers, the valleys, the desolate wastes, and the cities that are forsaken, which became a prey and derision to the residue of the heathen that are round about.

Daniel

In the third year of the reign of Jehoiakim king of Judah came Nebuchadnezzar king of Babylon unto Jerusalem and besieged it. The Lord gave Jehoiakim into his hand, with part of the vessels of the house of God: which he carried into the land of Shinar and into the treasure house of his god.

Nebuchadnezzar made an image of gold. Then the princes, governors, captains, and all the rulers of the provinces were gathered unto the dedication of the image the king had set up. An herald cried aloud, To you it is commanded, O people, nations, and languages, that at what time ye hear all kinds of musick, ye fall down and worship the image the king hath set up: whoso falleth not down and worshippeth shall the same hour be cast into the midst of a fiery furnace.

At that time certain Chaldeans accused the Jews. There are certain Jews thou hast set over the affairs of Babylon, Shadrach, Meshach, and Abednego; these men, O king, serve not thy gods, nor worship the image thou hast set up.

Nebuchadnezzar in his fury commanded to bring Shadrach, Meshach, and Abednego. They brought these men before the king. Nebuchadnezzar said, Is it true, do not ye worship the image I have set up?

Shadrach, Meshach, and Abednego answered, O Nebuchadnezzar, we are not careful to answer thee in this matter. If it be so, our God is able to deliver us from the furnace, and he will deliver us out of thine hand. But if not, be it known unto thee that we will not serve thy gods, nor worship the image thou hast set up.

Nebuchadnezzar commanded the most mighty men in his army to bind Shadrach, Meshach, and Abednego and cast them into the furnace. These three men fell down bound into the midst of the furnace. Then the king was astonished and said, I see four men loose, walking in the fire, and they have no hurt; and the fourth is like the Son of God.

Darius the Median took the kingdom. It pleased Darius to set over the kingdom three presidents; of whom Daniel was first. An excellent spirit was in him; and the king thought to set him over the whole realm. The presidents and princes sought to find occasion against Daniel concerning the kingdom; but they could find none. Then said these men, We shall not find any occasion against this Daniel, except we find it concerning the law of his God.

These presidents and princes assembled to the king and said, King Darius, establish a royal statute that whoever shall ask a petition of any God or man for thirty days, save of thee, shall be cast into the den of lions.

King Darius signed the decree.

When Daniel knew the writing was signed, he went into his house; his windows being open toward Jerusalem, he prayed and gave thanks before his God, as he did aforetime.

Then these men found Daniel praying and said before the king, Daniel regardeth not the decree thou hast signed.

The king, when he heard these words, was displeased with himself and set his heart on Daniel to deliver him.

These men said unto the king, No decree which the king

establisheth may be changed.

Then the king commanded, and they brought Daniel and cast him into the den of lions. The king said unto Daniel, Thy God whom thou servest continually will deliver thee.

The king arose very early in the morning and went unto the den of lions. He said, Daniel, is thy God able to deliver thee from the lions?

Then said Daniel, My God hath sent his angel and shut the lions' mouths, they have not hurt me.

Then was the king exceeding glad and commanded they take Daniel out of the den. The king commanded, and they brought those men which had accused Daniel and cast them into the den; and the lions had mastery of them.

King Darius wrote unto all people, I make a decree, That in every dominion of my kingdom men fear the God of Daniel: he is the living God, and his dominion shall be even unto the end.

Hosea

The word of the LORD that came unto Hosea son of Beeri in the days of Uzziah, Jotham, Ahaz, and Hezekiah, kings of Judah, and in the days of Jeroboam son of Joash, king of Israel.

The LORD said to Hosea, Go, take unto thee a wife of whoredoms and children of whoredoms: for the land hath committed great whoredom, departing from the LORD.

Then said the LORD unto me, Go, love a woman beloved of her friend, yet an adulteress, according to the love of the LORD toward the children of Israel, who look to other gods.

Hear the word of the LORD, children of Israel: for the LORD hath a controversy with the inhabitants of the land, because there is no truth nor mercy nor knowledge of God in the land.

Joel

The word of the LORD that came to Joel, son of Pethuel.

Hear this, old men, and give ear, all inhabitants of the land. That which the palmerworm hath left hath the locust eaten; and that which the locust hath left hath the cankerworm eaten; and that which the cankerworm hath left hath the caterpiller eaten.

I will restore to you the years that the locust hath eaten, the cankerworm, caterpiller, and palmerworm, my great army which I sent among you. Ye shall eat in plenty and be satisfied and praise the name of the LORD your God.

Amos

The days come, saith the LORD, that the plowman shall overtake the reaper, and the treader of grapes him that soweth seed; the mountains shall drop sweet wine, and all the hills shall melt.

I will bring again the captivity of my people of Israel, and they shall build the waste cities and inhabit them; they shall plant vineyards and drink the wine thereof; they shall make gardens and eat the fruit of them.

I will plant them upon their land, and they shall no more be pulled up out of their land I have given them, saith the LORD.

Obadiah

The vision of Obadiah concerning Edom: For thy violence against thy brother Jacob shame shall cover thee, and thou shalt be cut off for ever.

Jonah

The word of the LORD came unto Jonah, saying, Go to Nineveh and cry against it, for their wickedness. But Jonah rose to flee from the presence of the LORD and found a ship going to Tarshish.

The LORD sent a great wind so the ship was like to be broken. The mariners were afraid and said, What shall we do unto thee, that the sea may be calm?

He said, Cast me into the sea; for I know that for my sake this tempest is upon you.

Now the LORD had prepared a great fish to swallow Jonah. Jonah was in the fish three days.

Then Jonah prayed, and the LORD spake unto the fish, and it vomited Jonah upon dry land. Jonah arose, went unto Nineveh, and cried, Yet forty days, and Nineveh shall be overthrown. The people believed God. And God saw that they turned from their evil way.

But it displeased Jonah exceedingly. Then said the LORD, Should not I spare Nineveh, wherein are more than sixscore thousand persons?

Micah

I will look unto the LORD; I will wait for the God of my salvation. Rejoice not against me, O mine enemy: when I fall, I shall arise; when I sit in darkness, the LORD shall be a light unto me. I will bear the indignation of the LORD, because I have sinned against him, until he plead my cause and execute judgment for me: he will bring me forth to the light, and I shall behold his righteousness.

What doth the LORD require of thee but to do justly, love mercy, and walk humbly with thy God?

Nahum

The LORD is slow to anger and great in power and will not at all acquit the wicked: the LORD hath his way in the whirlwind and in the storm, and the clouds are the dust of his feet.

Habakkuk

The fig tree shall not blossom, neither shall fruit be in the vines; the labour of the olive shall fail, and the fields yield no meat; the flock shall be cut off from the fold, and there shall be no herd in the stalls: Yet I will rejoice in the LORD, I will joy in the God of my salvation.

Zephaniah

Seek ye the LORD, all ye meek of the earth, which have wrought his judgment; seek righteousness, seek meekness: it may be ye shall be hid in the day of the LORD's anger.

Haggai

Is the seed yet in the barn? yea, as yet the vine, fig tree, pomegranate, and olive tree hath not brought forth: from this day will I bless you.

Zechariah

In the second year of Darius came the word of the LORD unto Zechariah, saying, The LORD hath been displeased with your fathers. Therefore say unto them, Thus saith the LORD; Turn unto me, and I will turn unto you.

Thus speaketh the LORD, saying, Execute true judgment, shew mercy and compassions every man to his brother: oppress not the widow, nor the fatherless, the stranger, nor the poor; and let none of you imagine evil against his brother in your heart. But they stopped their ears, that they should not hear. Yea, they made their hearts as an adamant stone, lest they should hear the words the LORD of hosts sent by the former prophets: therefore came a great wrath from the LORD.

Malachi

Behold, the day cometh that shall burn as an oven; all the proud and all that do wickedly shall be stubble. But unto you that fear my name shall the Sun of righteousness arise with healing in his wings.

Matthew

Now the birth of Jesus Christ was on this wise: When his mother Mary was espoused to Joseph, before they came together, she was found with child of the Holy Ghost. Joseph her husband, being a just man and not willing to make her a public example, was minded to put her away privily.

But while he thought on these things, the angel of the Lord appeared unto him in a dream, saying, Joseph, son of David, fear not to take Mary thy wife: for that which is conceived in her is of the Holy Ghost. She shall bring forth a son, and thou shalt call his name JESUS: for he shall save his people from their sins.

All this was done, that it might be fulfilled which was spoken of the Lord by the prophet, saying, Behold, a virgin shall be with child and bring forth a son, and they shall call his name Emmanuel, which being interpreted is God with us.

In those days came John the Baptist, preaching in the wilderness of Judaea and saying, Repent: for the kingdom of heaven is at hand. This is he that was spoken of by the prophet Esaias [Isaiah], saying, The voice of one crying in the wilderness, Prepare ye the way of the Lord, make his paths straight.

Seeing the multitudes, he [Jesus] went up into a mountain: when he was set, his disciples came unto him: and he opened his mouth and taught them.

Lay not up for yourselves treasures upon earth, where moth and rust corrupts and where thieves break through and steal: but lay up for yourselves treasures in heaven, where neither moth nor rust doth corrupt and where thieves do not break through nor steal: for where your treasure is, there will your heart be also.

Enter in at the strait gate: for wide is the gate and broad the way that leadeth to destruction, and many go in thereat: strait is the gate and narrow the way which leadeth to life, and few find it.

Whosoever heareth these sayings of mine and doeth them, I will liken him unto a wise man which built his house upon a rock: the rain descended, the floods came, and the winds blew and beat upon that house; and it fell not: for it was founded upon a rock.

When Jesus had ended these sayings, the people were astonished: for he taught as one having authority, and not as the scribes.

Jesus went about all the cities and villages, teaching in their synagogues, preaching the gospel of the kingdom, and healing every sickness and disease among the people.
When he saw the multitudes, he was moved with compassion on them, because they fainted and were scattered abroad, as sheep

having no shepherd. Then saith he unto his disciples, The harvest is plenteous, but the labourers are few; pray therefore the Lord of the harvest, that he will send forth labourers into his harvest.

From that time forth began Jesus to shew unto his disciples how he must go unto Jerusalem, suffer many things of the elders and chief priests and scribes, be killed, and be raised again the third day.

Then Peter began to rebuke him, saying, Be it far from thee, Lord: this shall not be unto thee.

But he said unto Peter, Get behind me, Satan: thou art an offence unto me: for thou savourest not the things of God, but those of men.

Mark

Jesus took again the twelve and began to tell them what things should happen unto him, saying, Behold, we go up to Jerusalem; and the Son of man shall be delivered unto the chief priests and scribes; they shall condemn him to death and deliver him to the Gentiles: they shall mock him, scourge him, spit upon him, and kill him: and the third day he shall rise again.

When they came nigh to Jerusalem, unto Bethphage and Bethany, at the mount of Olives, he sendeth forth two of his disciples and saith unto them, Go into the village over against you: as soon as ye enter it, ye shall find a colt tied, whereon never man sat; loose him and bring him. And if any man say, Why do ye this? say that the Lord hath need of him; and straightway he will send him.

They brought the colt to Jesus and cast their garments on him; and he sat upon him. Many spread their garments in the way: others cut branches off the trees and strawed them in the way. They that went before and they that followed cried, Hosanna to the son of David: Blessed is he that cometh in the name of the Lord; Hosanna in the highest. Jesus entered into Jerusalem and into the temple: when he had looked round about upon all things and eventide was come, he went out unto Bethany with the twelve.

As he sat upon the mount of Olives over against the temple, Peter and James and John and Andrew asked him privately, Tell us, when shall these things be? and what shall be the sign when all these things shall be fulfilled?

Jesus began to say, Take heed lest any man deceive you: for many shall come in my name, saying, I am Christ; and shall deceive many. And when ye hear of wars and rumours of wars, be not troubled: for such things must be; but the end shall not be yet.

Luke

Now the feast of unleavened bread drew nigh, which is called the Passover. The chief priests and scribes sought how they might kill him [Jesus]; for they feared the people.

Then entered Satan into Judas Iscariot, being of the number of the twelve. He went his way and communed with the chief priests and captains, how he might betray him unto them.

Jesus went to the mount of Olives; and his disciples followed him. When he was at the place, he said unto them, Pray that ye enter not into temptation.

He was withdrawn from them about a stone's cast, and kneeled down and prayed, saying, Father, if thou be willing, remove this cup from me: nevertheless not my will, but thine, be done.

There appeared an angel unto him from heaven, strengthening him. Being in an agony he prayed more earnestly: and his sweat was as it were great drops of blood falling to the ground.

While he yet spake, behold a multitude, and Judas, one of the twelve, went before them and drew near unto Jesus to kiss him. But Jesus said, Judas, betrayest thou the Son of man with a kiss?

Then Jesus said unto the chief priests, captains of the temple, and elders, which were come to him, Be ye come out as against a thief, with swords and staves? When I was daily with you in the temple, ye stretched forth no hands against me: but this is your hour and the power of darkness. Then took they him and brought him into the high priest's house.

As soon as it was day, the elders of the people and the chief priests and scribes came together and led him into their council, saying, Art thou the Christ? tell us.

He said unto them, If I tell you, ye will not believe: and if I also ask you, ye will not answer me, nor let me go. Hereafter shall the Son of man sit on the right hand of the power of God.

Then said they all, Art thou then the Son of God?

He said, Ye say that I am.

They said, What need we any further witness? for we ourselves have heard of his own mouth.

Pilate, when he had called together the chief priests and the rulers and the people, said, Ye have brought this man unto me as one that perverteth the people: behold, I, having examined him before you, have found no fault in this man touching those things whereof ye accuse him.

They were instant with loud voices, requiring that he might be crucified. And the voices of them and of the chief priests prevailed. Pilate gave sentence that it should be as they required. He released unto them him that for sedition and murder was cast into prison, whom they had desired; but he delivered Jesus to their will.

As they led him away, they laid hold upon one Simon, a Cyrenian, coming out of the country, and on him they laid the cross, that he might bear it after Jesus. There were also two malefactors led with him to be put to death. When they were come to the place called Calvary, there they crucified him and the malefactors, one on the right hand and the other on the left. Then said Jesus, Father, forgive them; for they know not what they do.

It was about the sixth hour, and there was a darkness over all the earth until the ninth hour. The sun was darkened, and the veil of the temple was rent. When Jesus had cried with a loud voice, he said, Father, into thy hands I commend my spirit: having said thus, he gave up the ghost.

John

After this Joseph of Arimathaea, being a disciple of Jesus, besought Pilate that he might take away the body of Jesus: and Pilate gave him leave. He came therefore and took the body of Jesus. There came also Nicodemus, which at the first came to Jesus by night.

They took the body of Jesus and wound it in linen clothes with spices, as the manner of the Jews is to bury. Now in the place where he was crucified there was a garden; and in the garden a new sepulchre, wherein was never man yet laid. There laid they Jesus therefore because of the Jews' preparation day.

The first day of the week cometh Mary Magdalene early, when it was yet dark, unto the sepulchre, and seeth the stone taken away. She runneth to Simon Peter and the other disciple, whom Jesus loved, and saith to them, They have taken the Lord out of the sepulchre, and we know not where they have laid him.

Mary stood at the sepulchre weeping: and as she wept, she stooped down and looked into the sepulchre and seeth two angels in white sitting, one at the head, the other at the feet, where the body of Jesus had lain. They say unto her, Woman, why weepest thou?

She saith unto them, Because they have taken away my Lord, and I know not where they have laid him. When she had thus said, she turned and saw Jesus standing, and knew not that it was Jesus.

Jesus saith unto her, Woman, why weepest thou? whom seekest thou?

She, supposing him to be the gardener, saith unto him, Sir, if thou have borne him hence, tell me where thou hast laid him, and I will take him away.

Jesus saith unto her, Mary.

She turned and saith, Rabboni; which is to say, Master.

Jesus saith, Touch me not; for I am not yet ascended to my Father: but go to my brethren, and say unto them, I ascend unto my Father and your Father; to my God and your God.

Mary Magdalene told the disciples that she had seen the Lord and that he had spoken these things unto her.

Then the same day at evening, being the first day of the week, when the doors were shut where the disciples were assembled for fear of the Jews, came Jesus and stood in the midst and saith, Peace be unto you. When he had so said, he shewed them his hands and his side. Then were the disciples glad when they saw the Lord. Then said Jesus to them again, Peace be unto you: as my Father hath sent me, even so send I you.

Acts of the Apostles

Jesus, being assembled together with them, commanded them that they should not depart from Jerusalem, but wait for the promise of the Father, which ye have heard of me. For John truly baptized with water; but ye shall be baptized with the Holy Ghost not many days hence.

They asked, Lord, wilt thou at this time restore again the kingdom to Israel?

He said, It is not for you to know the times or the seasons, which the Father hath put in his own power. But ye shall receive power after the Holy Ghost is come upon you: and ye shall be witnesses unto me in Jerusalem and in all Judaea and in Samaria, unto the uttermost part of the earth.

When he had spoken these things, while they beheld, he was taken up; and a cloud received him out of their sight.

When the day of Pentecost was fully come, they were all with one accord in one place. Suddenly there came a sound from heaven as of a rushing mighty wind, and it filled the house where they were sitting. There appeared unto them cloven tongues as of fire, and it sat upon each of them. They were all filled with the Holy Ghost and began to speak with other tongues as the Spirit gave them utterance.

Peter, standing with the eleven, lifted up his voice and said, Men of Judaea and all that dwell at Jerusalem, be this known unto you, and hearken to my words: For these are not drunken, as ye suppose, seeing it is but the third hour of the day. But this is that which was spoken by the prophet Joel; And it shall come to pass in the last days, saith God,

I will pour out my Spirit upon all flesh: your sons and daughters shall prophesy, your young men shall see visions, and your old men shall dream dreams.

When they had prayed, the place was shaken where they were assembled; they were all filled with the Holy Ghost and spake the word of God with boldness. The multitude of them that believed were of one heart and one soul: neither said any of them that ought of the things he possessed was his own; but they had all things common. With great power gave the apostles witness of the resurrection of the Lord Jesus: and great grace was upon them all.

Saul, yet breathing out threatenings and slaughter against the disciples of the Lord, went unto the high priest and desired of him letters to Damascus to the synagogues, that if he found any of this way, whether men or women, he might bring them bound unto Jerusalem.

As he journeyed, he came near Damascus: and suddenly there shined round him a light from heaven: he fell to the earth and heard a voice saying unto him, Saul, Saul, why persecutest thou me?

He said, Who art thou, Lord?

And the Lord said, I am Jesus whom thou persecutest: it is hard for thee to kick against the pricks.

And he trembling and astonished said, Lord, what wilt thou have me to do?

The Lord said, Arise, go into the city, and it shall be told thee what thou must do.

There was a certain disciple at Damascus named Ananias; to him said the Lord in a vision, Ananias.

He said, Behold, I am here, Lord.

The Lord said unto him, Arise, go into the street called Straight, and enquire in the house of Judas for one called Saul, of Tarsus: for, behold, he prayeth and hath seen in a vision a man named Ananias coming in and putting his hand on him, that he might receive his sight.

Ananias answered, Lord, I have heard by many of this man, how much evil he hath done to thy saints at Jerusalem.

But the Lord said unto him, Go thy way: for he is a chosen vessel unto me, to bear my name before the Gentiles and kings and the children of Israel.

Saul, (who is also called Paul,) testified the kingdom of God, persuading them concerning Jesus, both out of the law of Moses and out of the prophets.

Romans

Paul, a servant of Jesus Christ, called to be an apostle, separated unto the gospel of God. I am not ashamed of the gospel of Christ: for it is the power of God unto salvation to every one that believeth; to the Jew first, and also to the Greek.

Therein is the righteousness of God revealed from faith to faith: as it is written, The just shall live by faith. For the wrath of God is revealed from heaven against all ungodliness and unrighteousness of men.

The righteousness of God is by faith of Jesus Christ unto all and upon all that believe: there is no difference: for all have sinned and come short of the glory of God; being justified freely by his grace through the redemption that is in Christ Jesus.

What shall we say then that Abraham our father, as pertaining to the flesh, hath found? For if Abraham were justified by works, he hath whereof to glory; but not before God. For what saith the scripture? Abraham believed God, and it was counted unto him for righteousness.

Being justified by faith, we have peace with God through our Lord Jesus Christ: by whom also we have access by faith into this grace wherein we stand, and rejoice in hope of the glory of God. Not only so, but we glory in tribulations also: knowing that tribulation worketh patience; patience, experience; and experience, hope: and hope maketh not ashamed; because the love of God is shed abroad in our hearts by the Holy Ghost given unto us.

1 Corinthians

Paul, called to be an apostle of Jesus Christ through the will of God, unto the church of God at Corinth: Grace be unto you from God our Father and the Lord Jesus Christ. I beseech you, brethren, by the name of our Lord Jesus Christ, that ye all speak the same thing and that there be no divisions among you; but that ye be perfectly joined together in the same mind and the same judgment.

I, brethren, when I came to you, came not with excellency of speech or of wisdom, declaring unto you the testimony of God. For I determined not to know any thing among you, save Jesus Christ and him crucified. My speech and preaching was not with enticing words of man's wisdom, but in demonstration of the Spirit and of power: that your faith should not stand in the wisdom of men but in the power of God.

Be followers of me even as I also am of Christ. I praise you, brethren, that ye remember me in all things and keep the ordinances as I delivered them to you.

Thanks be to God, which giveth us victory through our Lord Jesus Christ. Therefore, my beloved brethren, be ye stedfast, unmoveable, always abounding in the work of the Lord, as ye know that your labour is not in vain in the Lord.

2 Corinthians

We know that if our earthly house of this tabernacle were dissolved, we have a building of God, a house not made with hands, eternal in the heavens. For in this we groan, earnestly desiring to be clothed with our house which is from heaven: if so being clothed we shall not be found naked. For we that are in this tabernacle do groan, being burdened: not that we would be unclothed, but clothed, that mortality might be swallowed up of life. Now he that hath wrought us for the selfsame thing is God, who also hath given us the earnest of the Spirit. Therefore we are always confident, knowing that whilst we are at home in the body, we are absent from the Lord: (For we walk by faith, not by sight:) We are confident, I say, and willing rather to be absent from the body and present with the Lord.

If any man be in Christ, he is a new creature: old things are passed away; all things are become new.

Galatians

Paul, an apostle, and all the brethren with me, unto the churches of Galatia. I marvel that ye are so soon removed from him that called you into the grace of Christ unto another gospel: which is not another; but there be some that trouble you and would pervert the gospel of Christ. But though we or an angel from heaven preach any other gospel unto you than that which we have preached, let him be accursed.

Ephesians

Paul, an apostle of Jesus by the will of God, to the saints at Ephesus and to the faithful in Christ: By grace are ye saved through faith; it is the gift of God: Not of works, lest any man should boast.

Walk worthy of the vocation wherewith ye are called, with all lowliness and meekness, with longsuffering, forbearing one another in love; endeavoring to keep the unity of the Spirit in the bond of peace.

Be strong in the Lord and in the power of his might.

Philippians

Paul and Timotheus, servants of Jesus Christ, to all the saints in
Philippi: Rejoice in the Lord always: again I say, Rejoice. Let your
moderation be known unto all. The Lord is at hand. Be careful
for nothing; but in every thing by prayer and supplication with
thanksgiving let your requests be made known unto God. And the
peace of God, which passeth all understanding, shall keep your
hearts and minds through Christ Jesus.

Colossians

Paul, an apostle of Jesus to the saints and brethren at Colosse: If
ye be risen with Christ, seek those things which are above, where
Christ sitteth on the right hand of God. Set your affection on
things above, not on things on the earth. For ye are dead, and your
life is hid with Christ in God. When Christ, who is our life, shall
appear, then shall ye also appear with him in glory.

1 Thessalonians

Paul, and Silvanus, and Timotheus, unto the church of the
Thessalonians: We which are alive and remain unto the coming
of the Lord shall not prevent them which are asleep. For the Lord
himself shall descend from heaven with a shout, with the voice of
the archangel, and with the trump of God: the dead in Christ shall
rise first: then we which are alive and remain shall be caught up
together with them in the clouds to meet the Lord in the air.

2 Thessalonians

Brethren, pray for us, that the word of the Lord may have free course and be glorified, even as it is with you: and that we may be delivered from unreasonable and wicked men.

1 Timothy

Paul unto Timothy, my own son in the faith. This is a faithful saying and worthy of all acceptation, that Christ Jesus came into the world to save sinners; of whom I am chief. Howbeit for this cause I obtained mercy, that in me first Jesus Christ might shew forth all longsuffering, for a pattern to them which should hereafter believe on him to life everlasting. Now unto the King eternal, immortal, invisible, the only wise God, be honour and glory for ever and ever.

2 Timothy

God hath saved us and called us with an holy calling, not according to our works, but according to his own purpose and grace, which was given us in Christ Jesus before the world began, but is now made manifest by the appearing of our Saviour Jesus Christ, who hath abolished death and brought life and immortality to light through the gospel.

All scripture is given by inspiration of God, and is profitable for doctrine, reproof, correction, instruction in righteousness: That the man of God may be thoroughly furnished unto good works.

Titus

Paul, servant of God, to Titus, mine own son after the faith: The grace of God that bringeth salvation hath appeared to all men, teaching us that, denying ungodliness and worldly lusts, we should live soberly, righteously, and godly in this present world.

Philemon

Paul unto Philemon: I beseech thee for Onesimus in time past unprofitable, but now profitable to thee and to me: Receive him not now as a servant, but a brother beloved.

Hebrews

Let us labour to enter into that rest, lest any man fall after the same example of unbelief. For the word of God is quick, powerful, and sharper than any two-edged sword, piercing even to the dividing asunder of soul and spirit, and is a discerner of the thoughts and intents of the heart.

Let us therefore come boldly unto the throne of grace, that we may obtain mercy and find grace to help in time of need.

Let us draw near with a true heart in full assurance of faith, having our hearts sprinkled from an evil conscience and our bodies washed with pure water. Let us hold fast the profession of our faith without wavering; and let us consider one another to provoke unto love and good works.

Seeing we are compassed about with so great a cloud of witnesses, let us lay aside every weight and the sin which doth so easily beset us, and let us run with patience the race that is set before us, looking unto Jesus the author and finisher of our faith.

James

James, a servant of God and the Lord Jesus Christ, to the twelve tribes scattered abroad. Brethren, count it all joy when ye fall into divers temptations; knowing that the trying of your faith worketh patience. But let patience have her perfect work, that ye may be perfect and entire, wanting nothing.

The effectual fervent prayer of a righteous man availeth much.

1 Peter

Peter, apostle of Jesus Christ, to the elect: Blessed be the God and Father of our Lord Jesus Christ: whom having not seen, ye love; in whom ye rejoice with joy unspeakable and full of glory: receiving the end of your faith, even the salvation of your souls.

Forasmuch as Christ hath suffered for us in the flesh, arm yourselves likewise with the same mind: for he that suffered in the flesh hath ceased from sin; that he no longer should live his time in the flesh to the lusts of men, but to the will of God.

2 Peter

His divine power hath given us all things that pertain unto life and godliness through the knowledge of him that hath called us to glory and virtue: whereby are given unto us exceeding great and precious promises: that by these ye might be partakers of the divine nature, having escaped the corruption that is in the world through lust.

The Lord is not slack concerning his promise, as some men count slackness; but is longsuffering, not willing that any should perish but that all should come to repentance. The day of the Lord will come as a thief in the night; the heavens shall pass away with a great noise, and the elements shall melt with fervent heat, the earth and the works that are therein shall be burned.

1 John

That which we have seen and heard declare we unto you, that ye also may have fellowship with us: truly our fellowship is with the Father and his Son Jesus Christ.

My little children, these things write I to you that ye sin not. If any man sin, we have an advocate with the Father, Jesus Christ the righteous: he is the propitiation for our sins.

2 John

The elder unto the elect lady. Not as though I wrote a new commandment, but that which we had from the beginning, love one another.

3 John

The elder unto the well-beloved Gaius. I have no greater joy than to hear that my children walk in truth.

Jude

Jude, to them that are preserved in Jesus Christ. Ye should earnestly contend for the faith which was once delivered unto the saints. Keep yourselves in the love of God.

Revelation

The Revelation of Jesus Christ, which God gave unto him to shew his servants things which must shortly come to pass; he sent and signified it by his angel unto his servant John. Blessed is he that readeth and they that hear the words of this prophecy and keep those things written therein: for the time is at hand.

I was in the Spirit on the Lord's day and heard behind me a great voice, as of a trumpet, saying, I am Alpha and Omega, the first and the last: and, What thou seest, write in a book, and send it unto the seven churches in Asia; unto Ephesus, Smyrna, Pergamos, Thyatira, Sardis, Philadelphia, and Laodicea.

These sayings are faithful and true: and the Lord God of the holy prophets sent his angel to shew unto his servants the things which must shortly be done. Blessed is he that keepeth the sayings of the prophecy of this book. Behold, I come quickly; and my reward is with me, to give every man according as his work shall be.

Blessed are they that do his commandments, that they may have right to the tree of life and may enter in through the gates into the city. For without are dogs, sorcerers, whoremongers, murderers, idolaters, and whosoever loveth and maketh a lie.

I Jesus have sent mine angel to testify unto you these things in the churches. I am the root and the offspring of David, the bright and morning star. The Spirit and the bride say, Come. Let him that heareth say, Come. And let him that is athirst come. Whosoever will, let him take the water of life freely.

One Hundred and Fifty

Need-to-Know
Bible
Facts

Key Truths for Better Living

Ed Strauss

Contents

Introduction

You've probably already noticed—the Bible is a very large and complex book.

Actually, the Bible is a compilation of 66 "books," including histories, song collections, theological treatises, and personal letters. Written by some forty writers over hundreds of years, the Bible contains 1,189 chapters, more than 31,000 verses, and upwards of 780,000 words.

So how are we to make sense of it all? *150 Need-to-Know Bible Facts* can help.

This little book takes the great themes of the Bible and distills them into quick, easy-to-read entries to give you a bird's-eye view of scripture. Though every detail of the Bible is there for a reason, you'll probably find it most helpful to understand facts like

- God created everything.
- Sin is destructive.
- We are very important to God.
- Jesus' teachings are very simple.
- Faith can conquer fear.

These "need-to-know facts"—and 145 others like them—will walk you through the biggest, most important ideas of the Bible. You'll see the big picture, not only the individual brushstrokes.

We hope *150 Need-to-Know Bible Facts* will help you better understand the Bible—and better know the God who gave it to us.

THE EDITORS

1

God created *everything*.

In the beginning God created the heavens and the earth.
GENESIS 1:1

Look around you—where did everything come from? Sure, light came from the sun. . .trees grew from seeds. . .people were born to their mothers. But where did all those things originate *ultimately*? How did the sun take its place in the sky? Where did the very first seed-producing tree come from? How did your great, great, great (and so on) grandmother start the line of people that produced you?

Genesis 1 answers very simply: *God* made everything.

2

God simply *spoke* things into existence.

Then God said, "Let there be light";
and there was light.
GENESIS 1:3

Talented people make useful and beautiful things that enhance our lives—the houses we live in, the foods we eat, the art we enjoy. But every artisan must begin with some kind of raw material—wood, stone, grain, pigments. Not so with God.

When God wanted to create our incredible universe, He simply said the word—and it happened. Light, sky, dry land, plants, and animals. . .all arose at the command of the one true God. It's just one example of His amazing power.

3

In the beginning,
the world was perfect.

*Then God saw everything that He had made,
and indeed it was very good.*
GENESIS 1:31

The Garden of Eden was an astonishingly beautiful paradise,
but Eden was just part of the Big Picture. *All* of Creation on
the entire planet was "very good." All flora and fauna were flawless.
Our planet today is far from perfect. We live in a fallen world.
Disease and death, thorns and thistles have overtaken paradise.
And yet, pause for a moment, and you will still see so much beauty
shining through that it will take your breath away.

4

The devil caused doubt
and dissatisfaction.

*When the woman saw that the tree was. . .
desirable to make one wise, she took of its fruit and ate.*
GENESIS 3:6

Adam and Eve were living in Eden. They didn't have a problem or
a care. They should have been perfectly content, and they were—
that is, until the devil lied and "explained" that God had deceived them
in order to withhold the *best* from them. If they ate the forbidden fruit,
the serpent insisted, they would be wise like God.
   The only way to believe the devil was to disbelieve God—and
that's what Eve did. People have been falling for that same trick
ever since.

5

Sin is destructive.

For the wages of sin is death.
ROMANS 6:23

Adam and Eve's innocence was shattered the instant they disobeyed God. The sweet taste of the forbidden fruit was still on their tongues when its poison began its deadly work, quicker than a serpent's venom. Their minds were darkened, and they began seeing everything from a skewed, selfish perspective.

Worst of all, they died spiritually that day and began to die physically as well. The wages that their sin paid them was death.

Thankfully, God had already planned an antidote to the devil's poison.

6

Sin separates humanity from God.

Your iniquities have separated you from your God;
and your sins have hidden His face from you.
ISAIAH 59:2

Disobeying God came with a huge price: humanity's relationship with the divine was sundered. To this very day, mankind's iniquity separates us from God. We can no longer see His face. "We grope for the wall like the blind" (Isaiah 59:10).

When we have no relationship with the Lord, when the power lines are down, when doubt, denial, and disobedience leave us in darkness, how can we communicate with God? We can't.

Thankfully, God had already planned a way to turn the lights back on.

7

Man at his best is insignificant.

Behold, the nations are as a drop in a bucket,
and are counted as the small dust on the scales.
ISAIAH 40:15

We pride ourselves that we've come a long way. And we have. As magnificent as mankind's civilizations of the past were, think of the astonishing technologies of the modern world.

But none of our accomplishments can *begin* to compare to the eternal, omniscient God who created the vast universe, started every swirling galaxy turning, and said to every distant, giant star, "Be!"

The Bible pegs us accurately: our greatest nations are dust specks, and we're like microbes living on them.

8

We are *very* important to God.

What is man that You are mindful of him,
and the son of man that You visit him?
PSALM 8:4

Since God is the infinite Creator, who are *we* that He would care about us? Why would God even give humans a second thought—particularly since we rebelled against Him?

It is precisely because God *is* infinite that He can watch a distant asteroid, yet still notice when a hair from our head falls to the ground on earth. It is precisely because God *is* our Creator that He loves us—even in our fallen state.

And He has a wonderful plan for us.

9

The blood of sacrifices covered sin.

*"The life of the flesh is in the blood, and I have given it to
you upon the altar to make atonement for your souls."*
LEVITICUS 17:11

The punishment for sin is death, so when someone sinned,
legally, their blood had to be spilled. God allowed a substitute,
however. He ordained that His people sacrifice an animal to atone
for their sin. The Hebrew word for *atonement* means "to cover." In
a real spiritual sense, the blood of the lamb or goat covered over a
person's sin.

Every time someone sinned, however, they had to make
another sacrifice. . .and another. . . and another. Clearly, this was
only a temporary solution.

10

No one fully obeyed the Law of Moses.

*Whoever shall keep the whole law,
and yet stumble in one point, he is guilty of all.*
JAMES 2:10

To help people stay in loving relationship with Him and
others, God gave them the Law of Moses. This law contained
(according to the rabbis' count) 613 commandments—and people
had to obey them *all*. It wasn't enough to keep the command, "You
shall not commit adultery," but disobey, "You shall not gossip."

But people are only human, and the best of us trip up. (Try
giving generously and cheerfully to someone whom you know
won't repay.) As a result, no one kept the law perfectly.

11

God had a solution to sin.

God sent forth His Son...
to redeem those who were under the law.
GALATIANS 4:4–5

God was aware that even good-hearted, sincere people couldn't obey the law without fail—and that those who tried *hardest* to be righteous were often, well, self-righteous legalists. God was as displeased with merciless, unloving "righteousness" as He was with thoughtless, unloving sin.

For their part, the common people (whom the religious called "sinners") were aware of their failings, yet weary of trying to live up to impossible-to-keep standards.

The time was right, so God sent Jesus into the world with mercy and truth.

12

Jesus' life is a fact of history.

We did not follow cunningly devised fables when we made known to you
the power and coming of our Lord Jesus Christ, but were eyewitnesses.
2 PETER 1:16

The Gospels tell the facts of Jesus' birth, life, death, and resurrection. These aren't made-up fables like the insane adventures of the Greek gods. No, the powerful miracles the apostles describe actually happened! Peter, John, and Matthew were eyewitnesses.

In addition, tens of thousands of people from one end of Israel to the other had met Jesus and seen His miracles. As Paul pointed out, "This thing was not done in a corner" (Acts 26:26).

Make no mistake: the four Gospels are accurate historical reports.

13

Jesus is a perfect representation of God.

He is the image of the invisible God.
COLOSSIANS 1:15

T he Bible *tells* us that God has great love for us, but He knew
we were all basically from Missouri: we needed to be *shown*.
So God sent His only Son to earth to demonstrate what His love
was like.

Jesus was the perfect representation of God, and He
empathized with us and put up with everything we endure: hunger,
thirst, weariness, and temptation. By living among us, by caring for
us—then giving His very life—Jesus showed us that God indeed
loved us.

14

Jesus' blood completely cleanses us.

Jesus Christ. . .loved us and washed us
from our sins in His own blood.
REVELATION 1:5

W hen John the Baptist saw Jesus he shouted, "Behold! The
Lamb of God who takes away the sin of the world!" (John
1:29). He was right: Jesus was the final, perfect sacrificial lamb,
who offered His own lifeblood to save us.

Jesus' blood didn't just temporarily *cover* our sin like the blood
of sacrificial lambs had done. Jesus took our iniquities completely
away. His blood *washed away* our sins, leaving us clean. And He
did it *one* time, once and for all.

15

There's infallible proof that Jesus lives!

He also presented Himself alive after
His suffering by many infallible proofs.
ACTS 1:3

When Jesus appeared to His disciples after rising from the dead, they recognized Him all right, but thought they were seeing His ghost. So Jesus offered His disciples proof that it was really *Him*: He ate food and told them, "Touch Me."

That convinced them!

For the next forty days, before He ascended to heaven, Jesus appeared to over five hundred people and offered *many* and *infallible* proofs that He had indeed been resurrected from the dead. He wanted us to know that fact beyond all doubt.

16

Women were the first witnesses.

When He rose early on the first day of the week,
He appeared first to Mary Magdalene.
MARK 16:9

Two thousand years ago, Jewish religious leaders had a low opinion of women. Their testimony wasn't even accepted in a court of law; only male witnesses were believed. Yet all four Gospels report that *women* were the first to see Jesus alive again—and a formerly disreputable lady was first of all!

If the apostles had invented reports of seeing Jesus, they'd have surely claimed that one of *them* had seen Him. But the truth was what it was, so they told it like it happened.

17

The Gospels were written to inspire faith.

These are written that you may believe
that Jesus is the Christ, the Son of God.
JOHN 20:31

Many people think that the purpose of the Gospels is to inform us that an enlightened teacher named Jesus once walked the earth and advised us to love one another and do good— or that His miracles proved that He was some kind of holy man.

That's missing the main point by a country mile. John puts it succinctly: the *main* reason the Gospels were written was to cause us to believe that Jesus is God's Son—the only one who can give us eternal life.

18

God loved us at our worst.

God demonstrates His own love toward us,
in that while we were still sinners, Christ died for us.
ROMANS 5:8

Many of us secretly suspect that God only loves "good people" who've already got something going—and are already doing their best to love and obey Him. That's an easy mistake to slip into, but it *is* a mistake. God loves people who are still wallowing in sin, hurting themselves and others, and insisting that they don't even need God.

God sent His Son, Jesus, to make the ultimate sacrifice when we were totally undeserving and unappreciative of His immense love.

19

Our sin is utterly gone.

You will cast all our sins into the depths of the sea.
MICAH 7:19

Once you're forgiven, God doesn't hang on to a ledger listing your sins, pull it out every time you trip up, tap His fingers and say, "Just to let you know, I haven't forgotten these things." No. He says He has cast your sins—*all* your sins—into the Abyss, the deepest trench in the profoundest depths of the ocean, sunk to the utter bottom, never to be recovered.

Once your sins are forgiven, they are gone indeed, and you are forgiven indeed.

20

God has adopted us.

You received the Spirit of adoption by
whom we cry out, "Abba, Father."
ROMANS 8:15

We weren't God's sons and daughters to start with. We were like street urchins, grimy with sin, all our unrighteousness like filthy rags draped around us, homeless, destitute waifs. . .but then. . .

God adopted us as His own children, washed us clean, dressed us in robes of righteousness, and gave us the immense privilege of calling Him Father. We have been adopted into His family and warmly invited to sit at the royal table.

Oh, there are a few house rules. . .but we'll get to those.

21

Jesus literally lives in your heart.

God has sent forth the Spirit of His Son into your hearts.
GALATIANS 4:6

When you put your faith in Jesus Christ and ask Him to save you, His Spirit enters your heart—literally. This isn't just a figure of speech. God sends the Spirit of Jesus into your very being and He takes up residence there. He says, "I will dwell in them" (2 Corinthians 6:16).

You may argue that you're not "holy" enough for God to live in, that you're too much of a mess. But that's precisely why Jesus enters your life—to *make* you holy.

22

Only Jesus can save us.

Jesus said to him, "I am the way, the truth, and the life.
No one comes to the Father except through Me."
JOHN 14:6

We should respect other peoples' beliefs, but let's be very clear: Jesus stated that He is *the* truth, *the* life, and *the* only way to God. He is not one path among many. He is no optional side dish in the cafeteria of world beliefs.

Other religions teach *some* truth and may even lead *part*way to God, but Jesus is the only one who can save us, the only one who can get us completely across the yawning chasm of sin to the Father's arms.

23

We can now live Moses' law.

All the law is fulfilled in one word, even in this:
"You shall love your neighbor as yourself."
GALATIANS 5:14

It was a small command tucked away in a dry book of ceremonial laws. It wasn't even listed among the Ten Commandments. Yet these seven simple words in Leviticus 19:18—"You shall love your neighbor as yourself"—are the heart of the law.

The Law of Moses was strict and complicated. Jesus' message was merciful and simple: love God and love the person next to you. Do that and you just fulfilled all the requirements of the law.

Talk about keeping things simple!

24

We must love and obey God.

"That you may love the LORD your God, that you may obey His voice,
and that you may cling to Him, for He is your life."
DEUTERONOMY 30:20

Imagine that you must cross a swollen river. God can easily withstand the raging current, but all around you, you see debris being swept away. "Hold tightly to Me, My child," He says, and though you are afraid, you do. You obey His voice and cling to Him for your very life.

You must not only believe that He is strong enough to save you, but you must know that He loves you enough to actually do so. When you really "get" that, you will trust and love Him in return.

25

We must love one another.

Beloved, let us love one another, for love is of God;
and everyone who loves is born of God and knows God.
1 JOHN 4:7

Jesus said to love one another—even our enemies. (That surely includes family and friends at their crankiest.)

But why must we *love* them? Really, aren't we doing enough already if we manage to ignore them or to tolerate them? Why must we actually *love* them?

We must love others because love comes from God and God now lives in our heart. We love others because we are God's child. Loving others shows that we truly know God, and know who He is: love.

26

We love Jesus when we love others.

"Inasmuch as you did it to one of the least of
these My brethren, you did it to Me."
MATTHEW 25:40

We are to show love to others by doing tangible acts of kindness, doing what we can to meet their spiritual, emotional, and physical needs. But Jesus knew that some people weren't easy or convenient to love, so He emphasized that showing kindness to even the lowest person was showing it to *Him* personally.

Jesus loves every man, woman, and child on earth and strongly identifies with their pain, their sorrows, and their need for love. He wants us to feel that way, too.

27

We must put ourselves in others' shoes.

"Whatever you want men to do to you, do also to them."
MATTHEW 7:12

Moses' law commanded us to love our neighbor, but that raised the question, "Um. . .what am I supposed to *do* to show them love?" So Jesus turned it around and basically said, "Well think: how would you like others to treat *you*?"

The answer is: I'd like to be treated with respect, to be given the benefit of the doubt, to be helped when I need help, to be forgiven my mistakes, etc.

Well, there you have it! That's how you should treat others.

28

We must forgive others.

*"If you have anything against anyone,
forgive him, that your Father in heaven
may also forgive you your trespasses."*
MARK 11:25

We often think that if someone offends us, we can either choose to nobly forgive him or we can elect *not* to—that God will understand because, after all, that person really was/is a rotter.

Now, it often takes time to work through deep pain before we can forgive a serious offense. God knows that. He's helping us through that process. What God *doesn't* have time for, however, is us stubbornly hanging on to every trivial offense.

We ourselves need to be forgiven. Let's forgive others.

29

We need to *stretch* our love.

Above all things have fervent love for one another,
for "love will cover a multitude of sins."
1 PETER 4:8

Some people mentally assent to Jesus' command to love one another. Their love, however, has its definite limits. It generally holds up as long as the other person doesn't become *too* aggravating or cross them one too many times.

Peter clarified this, saying, "Have *fervent* love for one another." The Greek word for *fervent* means "stretched out." This kind of long-suffering, go-the-extra-mile love is the only kind that keeps on forgiving when the other person bugs you repeatedly.

30

Jesus' teachings are very simple.

I fear, lest somehow, as the serpent deceived Eve by his craftiness,
so your minds may be corrupted from the simplicity that is in Christ.
2 CORINTHIANS 11:3

Paul told the Christians of Corinth to beware if anyone rolled into town preaching "another Jesus"—a Jesus who suddenly had a bunch of requirements and regulations to help them save themselves. No matter how wise and sensible it seemed, it was like the serpent showing up to deceive Eve all over again!

The real Gospel message is simple. Not necessarily easy to live but certainly easy to grasp: believe on Jesus to be saved, love God, and love your fellow man. Period.

31

Even God's "foolish" ways are wise.

The foolishness of God is wiser than men,
and the weakness of God is stronger than men.
1 CORINTHIANS 1:25

The ancient Greeks were, like many people today, intellectual and philosophical. To them, inheriting heaven by faith in a bloodied, crucified Savior was foolishness. Surely the path to higher celestial states required secret wisdom, elevating one's spirit by an esoteric process of enlightenment.

The problem was—besides being wrong—that much of their "secret wisdom" was highly convoluted mental gymnastics. God's "simple foolishness" was far wiser than the vaunted tower of intellectual cards the Greeks had erected.

32

Christianity is a sane, reasonable faith.

"I am not mad, most noble Festus,
but speak the words of truth and reason."
ACTS 26:25

Many people suspect that putting their faith in Christ involves shutting down their brain and making a blind, emotional leap of faith in denial of everything that their rational mind *would* have told them had they not chosen to turn it off. Not so.

The Christian faith is based on truth. God exists. Christianity is based on actual historical facts. It is reasonable and true. It can stand the scrutiny of rational minds and bring even scholars and scientists to their knees.

33

Jesus' resurrection is credible.

*"Why should it be thought incredible
by you that God raises the dead?"*
ACTS 26:8

That God raises the dead to eternal life did not seem incredible to Paul two thousand years ago, and it should seem even *less* so to us today. After all, scientists recently discovered that a species of jellyfish ages *backward* and is *immortal*!

Think of other "impossibilities" of God's creation: life survives without oxygen in pools of sulphuric acid, thrives in scalding sub-oceanic vents, and lives in the arid, frozen valleys of Antarctica.

That God should raise the dead to life is a miracle, yes. . .but hardly incredible.

34

Luke accurately researched his Gospel.

*It seemed good to me also, having had perfect
understanding of all things from the very first,
to write to you an orderly account.*
LUKE 1:3

How do we know that the accounts of Jesus' life are accurate? Well, Matthew and John were eyewitnesses. And Luke is widely admitted to be one of the world's most trustworthy historians. He sailed to Israel to meticulously research the facts, interview witnesses, and write an orderly account of what happened.

The Gospels are not like those ludicrous magazines you see at the checkout stand. The Gospels are accurate historical reports. You can be certain that the events of Jesus' life happened just as recorded.

35

Christians are treasure seekers.

Search for her as for hidden treasures;
then you will understand the fear of the LORD,
and find the knowledge of God.
PROVERBS 2:4–5

You've seen those documentaries where treasure hunters spend years and use the most cutting-edge technology to search for lost treasure. Sometimes they strike pay dirt, and sometimes, well, they're still out there searching while the credits roll.

If you seek treasure in the Bible your spiritual Geiger counters will constantly be beeping and your dives will always be rewarded. Instead of finding doubloons, however, you'll be discovering wisdom for life and awesome truths about God.

36

God's Word is our spiritual food.

Your words were found, and I ate them,
and Your word was to me the joy and rejoicing of my heart.
JEREMIAH 15:16

Jesus said that man couldn't live by bread alone, but by every word that God speaks (Matthew 4:4).

Jeremiah said that he *ate* God's words. Of course, he wasn't literally chewing on a scroll, but the comparison is a good one. God's Word is our spiritual food.

It's not enough to merely find food, or to taste it. You must chew and digest it. That's when it gives you energy and life. And that's what happens when you read God's Word and "swallow" it down into your heart.

37

God's Word gives us faith.

Faith comes by hearing, and hearing by the word of God.
ROMANS 10:17

What do we do when we need more faith? We can pray for God to give us more, just like Jesus' disciples did when they said, "Increase our faith" (Luke 17:5). However, God has already supplied a surefire way for us to increase faith—by hearing and reading His Word.

Just as we build and strengthen muscles by spending time exercising, we build our faith by spending time reading the Bible and meditating on it. And we must read it regularly.

38

We need to check what the Bible says.

*They received the word with all readiness, and searched
the Scriptures daily to find out whether these things were so.*
ACTS 17:11

When Paul told his fellow Jews that Jesus was their long-awaited Savior, some rejected the claim without giving it a chance. Others who were more fair minded, however, listened carefully then did their own Bible research to check out what Paul was saying.

When someone teaches you something new, check it out with the Bible. Dig deep and see if it's so. They might be right and your life will be enriched. Or you might find out that's *not* what the Bible teaches.

Either way, check it out.

39

We don't know better than the Bible.

*"Behold, they have rejected the word of the LORD;
so what wisdom do they have?"*
JEREMIAH 8:9

Some of the world's wisest people are *not* very informed when it comes to God and the Bible. They're highly focused on their particular area of expertise, but they're novices when it comes to spiritual matters. As long as they admit their limitations, it's not a problem.

The danger comes when they suppose their intelligence makes them wiser than God's Word. But what does a degree in, say, astrophysics count for when most of the questions on the exam are about man's relationship to God?

40

The Holy Spirit helps us.

*"The Holy Spirit. . .will teach you all things, and bring
to your remembrance all things that I said to you."*
JOHN 14:26

Jesus sent His Holy Spirit to dwell in our hearts and minds. Think of the Spirit as an all-wise, live-in tutor—a teacher who knows the answer to every question. The Spirit of God is God Himself. No wonder He can teach us "all things."

One of the most usual ways the Spirit teaches us is by reminding us of the things Jesus said. Of course, we have to first *read* Jesus' words in the Bible. Then He can bring them *back* to our memory.

41

God's Spirit gives us love.

The love of God has been poured out in our
hearts by the Holy Spirit who was given to us.
ROMANS 5:5

Jesus taught that the only way to fulfill the Law of Moses was to love God with all our hearts and to love our fellow man as much as we love ourselves. It sounds simple, but actually *living* it is a very tall order!

How on earth can we do that? Humanly, we don't *have* that much love.

The solution: God gives it to us! God *is* love, and when His Spirit fills us, He pours out the love of God in our hearts.

42

The Holy Spirit gives us power.

"You shall receive power when the Holy Spirit has
come upon you; and you shall be witnesses to Me."
ACTS 1:8

Perhaps you've heard the saying, "The Holy Spirit gives us power to live the Christian life." This is true. God wants you to live Jesus' teachings, yet He is aware that you can't do it by yourself. But when His Spirit empowers you, you *can.*

And when people around you see true Christianity in action, it inspires them to believe in God. Your very life becomes a witness. The Holy Spirit also empowers you to speak out and tell others how Jesus has changed your life.

43

The Spirit grows virtues in us.

The fruit of the Spirit is love, joy, peace, longsuffering,
kindness, goodness, faithfulness, gentleness, self-control.
GALATIANS 5:22–23

The "fruit" of the Spirit is the virtues that God grows in a
Christian's life. They won't spring forth at once, fully grown.
However, once the Spirit enters, they begin to grow. They are
in stark contrast to natural vices such as "lewdness. . .jealousies,
outbursts of wrath, selfish ambitions," etc. (Galatians 5:19–20).

This doesn't mean that if you still struggle with anger you're
not saved. But it does mean that if you allow God to change you,
your virtues will replace your vices.

44

Jesus' mother gave good advice.

His mother said to the servants,
"Whatever He says to you, do it."
JOHN 2:5

When Mary and Jesus were at a marriage in Cana, the host
ran out of wine. Mary turned to the servants and said,
"Whatever He says to you, do it." Jesus then told them to fill up
the water jugs. They obeyed, and He turned the water into wine.

This command sums up our Christian duty. Sometimes,
what Jesus tells us to do makes little sense at first. Sometimes He
commands us to do something difficult. But if He says to do it, we
should *do* it.

45

Obeying Jesus proves we love Him.

"If you love Me, keep My commandments."
JOHN 14:15

Christians are to love Jesus. And how do we know if we *actually* love Him? Because we have warm feelings when we think about Him? Well, that's a good start. But contrary to songs on the radio, true love is not just emotions or an endorphin rush.

When you truly love someone, you're willing to do anything for them. When they ask you a favor, why, you roll up your sleeves.

Jesus said, "Keep My commandments." So let's put our love into action.

46

We must lose our lives for Jesus.

"He who finds his life will lose it, and he who loses his life for My sake will find it."
MATTHEW 10:39

Many people seek the things of this life first and foremost. They focus on the material goods and the pleasures of this world, and though they may *get* a comfortable life, they lose something infinitely more valuable in the process—their spiritual life.

Christians may seem to "lose out" by making sacrifices because they're determined to put Jesus first and love others. But in reality, by living unselfishly, they *find* life in all its fullness—both in this world and in the world to come.

47

We must be nonconformists.

Do not be conformed to this world, but be
transformed by the renewing of your mind.
ROMANS 12:2

Many of us like to think that we're nonconformists, but often we're as caught up in the lemming mentality as the person next to us. We find ourselves subscribing to the lifestyle and mind-set and blogs of one crowd or another.

The pull of the world is so strong that it's an ongoing struggle to avoid being sucked into it. The best way is to let God's Spirit transform us. He does that by renewing our minds while we're reading the Bible and praying.

48

Sins of omission are sins.

Therefore, to him who knows to do good
and does not do it, to him it is sin.
JAMES 4:17

Hurting others—whether willfully or through a lack of concern—is wrong. We all know that. But there are sins of omission as well as sins of commission. Is there a lonely shut-in you've been avoiding visiting? An act of kindness you've been meaning to do? A blank on the volunteer list where your name would fit nicely?

Failure to do small things seems almost too insignificant to count as sins—but they *are* sins. Do something on God's "To Do" list today.

49

We will reap what we sow.

Whatever a man sows, that he will also reap.
GALATIANS 6:7

Many people, when something bad happens, chalk it up to so-called karma, "cause and effect." Nonsense. The principle of "you reap what you sow" comes straight from the Bible.

Paul is speaking here about eternity: if we sow to the Spirit, we'll reap everlasting life. But this principle surely applies to things in this life also. Selfish, unloving actions—unless we repent of them—have a way of coming back to us. But the happy news is this: whatever good we do will return to bless us.

50

We must allow God to prune us.

"Every branch in Me that. . .bears fruit He prunes,
that it may bear more fruit."
JOHN 15:2

Jesus compared Himself to a grapevine and us to individual branches. When we're joined to Jesus, we bear good fruit—Christian virtues, good deeds, and a life that's a witness to others.

If any branch is dead, God simply lops the whole thing off. But if any parts of a *living* branch are using up sap but not bearing fruit, He pulls out His pruning shears and snips those suckers off.

We need to allow God to cut sins and bad habits out of our life.

51

We must get rid of our garbage.

Turn away my eyes from looking at worthless things,
and revive me in Your way.
PSALM 119:37

Here's a guy who was honest enough to admit that he lacked the willpower to turn his eyes away from desiring worthless things. So he asked God to help him. Another thing: he was *trying* to walk in God's path, but he'd been fumbling recently.

"Revive me! Give me a personal revival!" That's a prayer that we all do well to pray. And revival often begins with a sincere desire to bag up the garbage in our lives and put it out on the curb.

52

God searches our hearts.

Search me, O God. . .and see if there is any wicked
way in me, and lead me in the way everlasting.
PSALM 139:23–24

When we pray this prayer, we open up all our doors and dresser drawers and give God permission to go through and search out any sins. Mind you, God *already* knows us well. But this invites Him to bring these sins to our attention and have a heart-to-heart chat about them.

God doesn't do this to make us despair at how bad we are, but because He loves us. He wants to get rid of anything that hinders us from walking "in the way everlasting."

53

Living in love is being full of God.

You, being rooted and grounded in love. . .
may be filled with all the fullness of God.
EPHESIANS 3:17, 19

We all wish for more of God's presence in our life, but secretly fear it. We suspect that experiencing God fully only happens to missionaries in foreign lands—which we are not—or to wide-eyed fanatics—which we'd rather avoid.

But the truth is more ordinary and closer to home: We are to live a life filled with love. We must send our roots deep down into love and build on it as a foundation. It's a lifelong process, but we can begin today.

54

Living God's Word frees us.

"If you abide in My word. . .you shall know
the truth, and the truth shall make you free."
JOHN 8:31–32

We're familiar with the saying, "The truth shall make you free," and apply it to a number of things. Indeed, knowing the truth about a situation in your childhood, or *who* said what to whom yesterday, can be liberating. . .or at least a relief.

But if you want to be truly liberated, you must get your head around what Jesus was saying: only knowing and living *His* words will actually set you free. And you must *abide in*—continue living—the truths Jesus taught.

55

God commands us not to gossip.

"You shall not go about as a talebearer among your people."
LEVITICUS 19:16

God made us social creatures who need to share what's
happening in our lives and families, and to catch up on the
news about others. Yet He commands us not to gossip—spread
tales about others—even if they're *true* tales.

How can we avoid crossing the line from chatting to
gossiping? Well, if we love the person we're talking about, we'll use
more discretion when deciding how much, if anything, we say. And
while *some* people need to know the details, not everybody does.

56

God commands us to be honest.

"These are the things you shall do:
Speak each man the truth to his neighbor."
ZECHARIAH 8:16

We expect others to be honest with us in everyday dealings.
We deeply admire those who are honest when honesty costs
them or is embarrassing. After all, we ourselves sometimes struggle
whether to 'fess up or not.

But "honesty is the best policy," as they say.

Honesty is not just the *best* policy, however. It's literally a
commandment. Exodus 20:16 tells us to not bear witness against
our neighbor. That's one of the ten "you shall *nots*." This is one of
the "you shall *do*" commands.

57

Shortchanging others is stealing.

"You shall not cheat your neighbor, nor rob him."
LEVITICUS 19:13

We're appalled at the thought of breaking into our neighbor's house and robbing him—which is a fortunate thing. But we shouldn't cheat or shortchange our neighbors, either. (And remember: everyone is our neighbor.)

That means, for example, that we shouldn't take advantage of anyone's ignorance and sell them an overrated product or dump damaged goods on them. If we're selling a used car that has problems, we should disclose those problems.

We wouldn't sell a bum steer to Jesus, so we shouldn't do it to others.

58

We must return lost items.

"If you meet your enemy's ox or his donkey going astray, you shall surely bring it back to him again."
EXODUS 23:4

You get a rush out of returning lost items to those you *love*, right? You smile broadly as you hand it over, thoroughly enjoying their relief and profuse thanks. It feels good!

But when it comes to strangers, we're sometimes tempted to apply the saying, "Finders keepers, losers weepers." Or when it comes to those who hate us, we might even feel a twinge of pleasure as we let their donkey amble by.

Don't. God says go out of your way to return it.

59

We should be kind and affectionate.

Be kindly affectionate to one another with brotherly love,
in honor giving preference to one another.
ROMANS 12:10

It's one thing to say, "Love one another." It's really closing all the loopholes to say, "Be *kindly affectionate* to one another." Otherwise you'd *love* quite a few people but not particularly like them. To be "kindly affectionate," however, implies that you actually *like* loving them.

As if that weren't enough, this verse takes everything one step further: you are to honor fellow believers—treat even the lowliest with respect. When you do that, you end up being kind and affectionate to everyone.

60

Christians should be united.

That you all speak the same thing,
and that there be no divisions among you. . .
1 CORINTHIANS 1:10

Verses like this have been used to argue that unity consists of everyone, like one giant chorus, all speaking the exact same thing on every issue. This is not unity but mere conformity. The humorous catch is that churches who demand such "unity" believe that *they* have it right and everyone should agree with *them*.

We should definitely "speak the same thing" on the basic tenets of the faith. However, Christian charity dictates that we not despise fellow believers who disagree on secondary issues.

61

God wants us to attend church.

Let us consider one another in order to stir up love and good
works, not forsaking the assembling of ourselves together.
HEBREWS 10:24–25

There are many good reasons to attend church faithfully. For one, there is beauty and power in united worship. For another, the pastor might motivate you with a good message. And then there's the chance to admire the sea of colorful Easter bonnets.

Seriously. . .attending church is also a great time to connect with fellow believers, to encourage one another, to pray for one another, and to stir each other up to live as Christians. You attend church not just for yourself but for others, too.

62

Shameless self-promotion backfires.

It is not good to eat much honey;
so to seek one's own glory is not glory.
PROVERBS 25:27

Why isn't it good to eat too much honey? Well, it seems great at first—like any very rich dessert—but as Proverbs 25:16 says, the person who eats a whole lot of honey ends up *sick* of it.

It's the same thing with someone who constantly tries to attract attention and get people to admire them—they get a reputation as a braggart and a show-off.

There's nothing wrong with sincere praise. Just don't go out of your way to *seek* it.

63

Mere knowledge can bloat us.

We know that we all have knowledge.
Knowledge puffs up, but love edifies.
1 CORINTHIANS 8:1

As Christians, we should study the Bible and seek to grow in the faith—but growing spiritually is not the same thing as memorizing Bible trivia and packing away knowledge. Merely filling our head with facts will bloat our ego into some unnatural shape—*puff* us up. But having love will edify us—*build* us up.

Bible facts and trivia can be interesting and fun, but if we are to be built solidly to last, let's grow in love for God and others.

64

We must avoid conceit.

Do not set your mind on high things, but associate with
the humble. Do not be wise in your own opinion.
ROMANS 12:16

Ah yes, conceit. We're all prone to it in certain areas. We have lofty opinions of ourselves and high expectations of what we'll do. We're convinced that we're wise and we speak our opinions with confidence, certain that we're right.

Pride is a common human vice. That's why the Bible cautions us to not be self-absorbed, nor to admire our own wisdom, but to come down and rub shoulders with humble, ordinary people.

After all, we're really rather ordinary ourselves.

65

We *should* desire to be great.

"Whoever desires to become great among you
shall be your servant."
MARK 10:43

There's nothing wrong with desiring to be great—as long as it's true greatness one desires. True greatness means humbly serving others, because one esteems others to be better than himself (Philippians 2:3). When someone has that attitude, they've attained greatness.

Those who are great in God's eyes don't *think* that they're so hot. They're very aware of their weaknesses and failings. It's not that they have an inferiority complex; they've simply taken a sober look at themselves.

We should desire that kind of greatness.

66

We can do nothing of ourselves.

"I am the vine, you are the branches. He who abides in Me, and I in
him, bears much fruit; for without Me you can do nothing."
JOHN 15:5

Jesus said, "Without Me you can do *nothing*," yet ungodly people often do well in this life—they build successful businesses and own nice houses and cars. Jesus was saying, however, that unless we're joined to Him, we have zero hope of eternal life. The sap of His Spirit in us causes us to bear "fruit"—virtues, good works, etc.—but we can't do that on our own.

People *can* be successful in this brief life, true, but if they're not alive spiritually, they and all that they do amounts to nothing.

67

It's best to get angry *slowly*.

Let every man be swift to hear,
slow to speak, slow to wrath.
JAMES 1:19

If you have a quick temper, you might be thinking, Right. *"Be slow to wrath." If only it were that easy.* Well, it may not be easy, but it can be done.

James *first* says to do two things to throw a wet blanket on a hot temper: first, be quick to hear the other person out. Don't jump to conclusions. Second: be slow to speak. Bite your tongue. Don't engage your mouth too quickly.

James's tips are guaranteed to slow down a quick temper.

68

Arguing is often utterly pointless.

"How forceful are right words!
But what does your arguing prove?"
JOB 6:25

There's no arguing the fact that reasonable words are more effective than pointless arguing. (Well, a person could dispute that, but they'd only be proving its point.)

Disagreements are to be expected, but too often they develop into emotional exchanges. Tempers flare, voices are raised, and the only thing anyone manages to prove is that two people are talking and, apparently, no longer listening.

We mistakenly feel that heated arguments are "forceful." But surprise! They're really not. Gently spoken reasons are what truly convince people.

69

God hates evil thoughts.

*"Let none of you think evil in your heart against your neighbor. . . .
For all these are things that I hate," says the Lord.*
Zechariah 8:17

There are valid reasons to be angry, but Jesus surprised a lot of people by saying that if they were angry at a person without a cause they'd be judged as if they'd committed murder. If they lusted they were already guilty of adultery (Matthew 5:21–30).

They shouldn't have been surprised. God has *always* been concerned with the quality of our brain waves. After all, murders begin with angry intentions, and adultery begins with silent lust. Stop the evil thoughts and the evil deeds won't happen.

70

Don't seek revenge.

*See that no one renders evil for evil to anyone,
but always pursue what is good.*
1 Thessalonians 5:15

We understand about not paying back evil to someone who has done evil to us because evil is, well, evil. And Christians don't do evil. But any kind of revenge, however petty, is bad. (You couldn't call it "pursuing good," could you?)

Solomon said, "Do not say, 'I will do to him just as he has done to me'" (Proverbs 24:29). That means that even "getting even" or "tit for tat" is out.

Let's do what the Bible *says*: let's do what is *good* in return.

71

Getting even messes things up.

Do not avenge yourselves. . .for it is written,
"Vengeance is Mine, I will repay," says the Lord.
ROMANS 12:19

W hy *shouldn't* we get back at those who wrong us? Well, God
wants us to love others in the hope that they'll repent and
change. . .but us getting revenge on them shows them we hate
them and haven't forgiven them. When we hurt them in return,
they get our message loud and clear.

Let's not send the wrong message.

If love and kindness doesn't wake them up, but they keep on
offending, be sure that God will eventually take vengeance on them.

72

Gloating over your enemy is self-defeating.

Do not rejoice when your enemy falls. . .
lest the LORD see it, and it displease Him,
and He turn away His wrath from him.
PROVERBS 24:17–18

O kay, so your enemy doesn't repent despite your continued
kindness. You leave him in God's hands and sure enough,
the day of retribution finally arrives. You hear he's injured in an
accident or is about to declare bankruptcy. Whatever you do, do
not gloat. Do not rejoice. You're supposed to *love* him, remember?

Keep your fingers completely out of God's wheels of justice.
The day He finally brings retribution on your enemy, God will be
watching *your* heart and your reactions closely.

73

It pays to start the day with prayer.

To You I have cried out, O LORD, and in
the morning my prayer comes before You.
PSALM 88:13

From the moment we wake up, we're already mulling yesterday's unresolved problems and trying to solve them. And we're faithful to jumpstart our brain with a cup of coffee. (We need to, right?)

And yes, we discuss the day's business with coworkers. (To get on top of things.)

But if we *really* want to hit the ground running, we simply must set aside some time every morning to pray. If we take the time to commit our day to God, it will make such a difference!

74

Faithful, daily prayer is vital.

He sought God. . .and as long as he sought
the LORD, God made him prosper.
2 CHRONICLES 26:5

Uzziah became king of Judah after an invasion and financial calamity. He brought Judah up from the ashes of defeat and made it even stronger than before. He reigned for fifty-two years. God blessed him and prospered him mightily because Uzziah was in the habit of praying about things. He was constantly seeking God.

This same principle still works today. Faithfully praying about our problems won't immediately banish them, but God will work *for* and *with* us and give us victory over things we face.

75

We must meditate on God.

And Isaac went out to meditate in the field in the evening.
GENESIS 24:63

Isaac was a wealthy patriarch, head of a sheep- and goat-herding empire in southern Canaan. He daily dealt with the details of a huge "business," and had to be both diplomatic and ready to defend. This involved a lot of thought and decisions. No wonder he took time out.

Like Isaac, let's be in the habit of meditating after the day's work—and take time from our busy schedule to unwind, to enjoy a sunset, and to meditate on God.

76

God *wants* to answer our prayers.

Delight yourself also in the LORD, and He
shall give you the desires of your heart.
PSALM 37:4

We often remind God of this promise when we want Him to grant our heart's desires. "After all," we say, "I love God. I delight myself in Him."

There's another condition, however. Note the word *also*. The *previous* verse says we must "trust in the Lord." It's quite simple, really: when we delight in God, we trust that He knows what's best, and we are delighted to allow Him to overrule us if what our hearts desire isn't actually *so* good for us.

77

We must pray within God's will.

This is the confidence that we have in Him, that if we ask anything according to His will, He hears us.
1 JOHN 5:14

God will grant us good things so long as those things are within His will. Often, however, we pray for things that aren't what God wants for us. After all—honestly now—if He *did* give us a problem-free life or let us be utterly secure financially, how would we learn to trust Him, turn to Him in prayer, or grow spiritually?

If something is God's will, we can expect Him to answer our prayer—but we must sincerely say, "Your will be done" (Matthew 6:10).

78

We must have faith when we pray.

"Whatever things you ask in prayer, believing, you will receive."
MATTHEW 21:22

Many people pray for something they actually need—which is certainly God's will for them—yet have little faith that He'll actually answer prayer. They pray because, well, praying is "what Christians do."

Often, they don't believe when they pray because they doubt that God has the power to do miracles in this day and age. Or they struggle to believe that He *loves them* enough to give them what they need.

God definitely has the power. And He definitely loves you.

79

When we obey, God answers prayer.

Whatever we ask we receive from Him,
because we keep His commandments and
do those things that are pleasing in His sight.
1 JOHN 3:22

Sometimes we lack faith that God will answer our prayer because we have this niggling feeling that we're disobeying Him somehow. That "niggling feeling" is God's Spirit speaking to our conscience. We want to ignore it and proceed directly to our prayer requests, but prayer is not just us talking to God. It's two-way communication in a relationship.

Let's listen to God and make things right. When our relationship is restored, He'll be happy to listen to us and give us what we pray for.

80

Jesus constantly prays for us.

It is Christ who. . .is even at the right hand of God,
who also makes intercession for us.
ROMANS 8:34

Jesus is now in heaven, seated at the right hand of His Father. But He's not just sitting there, micromanaging the entire universe. His mind is still very much on us, and He constantly intercedes with God on our behalf.

What kinds of things is He requesting for us? Well, while He was on earth, He said of Simon, "I have prayed for you, that your faith should not fail" (Luke 22:32). So it's a fair guess that He's still most interested in our spiritual welfare.

81

God speaks through the Bible.

Open my eyes, that I may see
wondrous things from Your law.
PSALM 119:18

What's the best way to find God's will? Instead of expecting Him to give you an outstanding sign or speak in an audible voice, read your Bible. It *is* God's Word, after all, what He's already said. When it commands, "Don't steal," well, that *settles* the matter.

Sometimes you read and reread a chapter, however, but until God opens your eyes, you don't see an amazing truth right in front of you—at least you don't *get* it.

That's why you must pray before reading.

82

We must know what the Bible says.

"You are mistaken, not knowing the
Scriptures nor the power of God."
MATTHEW 22:29

Have you ever looked for the verse, "Don't rob Peter to pay Paul"? You didn't find it because it's not in the Bible. Mistakes like that can be embarrassing, but people make more serious mistakes by assuming that the Bible backs up their personal beliefs—when it says nothing of the sort.

We can't afford to be mistaken about important issues or ignorant of what the scriptures say. Begin faithful, *daily* Bible reading today. You'll learn some amazing things about God!

83

We must *not* go to mediums.

When they say to you, "Seek those who are mediums. . . ,"
should not a people seek their God?
ISAIAH 8:19

You'd be surprised at how many people who "believe in God"
consult a psychic to find out what to do. After all, God is
silent *just* when they need to know who to marry or whether to
give a loan to their cousin.

Or they sneak a peek at their daily horoscope "just in case." Or
they read their fortune cookie and take it quite seriously.

Seek God and wait for Him to show you what to do. The wait
is worth it.

84

We must listen to godly counselors.

Without counsel, plans go awry, but in the multitude
of counselors they are established.
PROVERBS 15:22

When you pray for God's wisdom, God may give *you* that
wisdom. . .or He may give it to someone *else*. So don't try
to figure everything out yourself. You need the input that godly
men or women can give—especially pastors and older saints who've
walked many years with God and know how He deals with people.

Get a second and third and fourth opinion just to be sure. Seek
out godly advice. . .and listen to it carefully.

85

God *can* reveal His will clearly.

Cause me to know the way in which I should walk,
for I lift up my soul to You.
PSALM 143:8

Sometimes you need specific direction, and though you've read your Bible, no verse jumped out at you. You've counseled with godly people, but the best they offer is to pray for you. Well, that's what *you* should be doing, too!

Sometimes you need to pray desperately for God to make it plain which way you should turn. If it's a serious decision, fasting will help you give the Lord your undivided attention.

If you pray wholeheartedly, God will answer (Jeremiah 33:3).

86

The Bible commands us to work for a living.

Work with your own hands, as we commanded you. . .
that you may lack nothing.
1 THESSALONIANS 4:11–12

It's important that Christians have a strong work ethic: doing an honest day's work is a large part of our Christian witness. After all, most of us spend much of our waking hours in the workplace. That's where we're called to live out our faith.

There's another obvious reason for working diligently: it pays the bills. Otherwise we end up doing without, or borrowing to make ends meet.

Working is such an integral part of Christianity that Paul made it a commandment.

87

God gives us power
to earn money.

*"You shall remember the LORD your God,
for it is He who gives you power to get wealth."*
DEUTERONOMY 8:18

Like so many people today, if the Israelites acquired riches or prospered, they tended to pat themselves on the back and give themselves credit. God warned them against thinking that their skill or shrewdness had brought them wealth.

They *had* power to get wealth, true, but where did that power come from? *God.* We may be the ones sweating, but God is the one who gives us marketable skills, supplies us with work, and causes us to prosper.

88

Wealth can be dangerous.

*"The cares of this world and the deceitfulness of
riches choke the word, and he becomes unfruitful."*
MATTHEW 13:22

Riches can be good if handled responsibly and used for God's kingdom, and many Christians promise that they will do exactly that if *only* God would make them wealthy. But riches are very deceitful and cunning enough to ensnare those who "own" them.

If you acquire wealth, don't transfer your trust from God to your bank account, and don't become preoccupied with material things. Gold and goods are beautiful, yes, but not if they overrun you like weeds and choke out your spiritual life.

89

You must commit plans to God.

Unless the LORD builds the house,
they labor in vain who build it.
PSALM 127:1

When you build a house—or a business, or start any project—it involves a lot of work. But don't forget to include God in your planning, or you'll be doing all that work in vain. Without His blessing, you're basically piling up bricks without cement.

It's not enough to assume that your plans please God because they please you. You must spread your blueprints out before the Almighty and give Him veto power. And if you *do* build, build according to His principles.

90

We must be committed to God.

I have learned both to be full and to be hungry,
both to abound and to suffer need.
PHILIPPIANS 4:12

Many couples vow to be true to their spouse "for rich or for poor," because no one can really predict what your future holds. In lean financial times, people relearn the value of such a commitment. If it remains strong, it can sustain their marriage.

We must also remain committed to the Lord no matter what ups and downs we encounter in life. Whether God has us rich or poor, whether we abound or suffer need, let us determine to remain true to God.

91

Worldly gain is no gain at all.

Godliness with contentment is great gain.
For we brought nothing into this world,
and it is certain we can carry nothing out.
1 TIMOTHY 6:6–7

What makes a man truly rich? Winning the lottery? A lifetime of shrewd investments that deliver huge dividends? Owning a mansion and a yacht? No. After all, when he leaves this world, he can't take those gains into eternity. . .so what actual "gain" are they?

Living close to God, becoming more like Him, and being content with what we have. . .that is *truly* great gain.

Godliness and contentment we *can* take out of this world with us.

92

God owns everything on earth.

For every beast of the forest is Mine,
and the cattle on a thousand hills.
PSALM 50:10

God owns the entire earth and every creature on it. We don't have a problem with Him owning the wild beasts—after all, He *created* them. And, moreover, we're not using them. But we find it unsettling that God claims that all domestic cattle are His also. We thought they were *our* property.

But God goes further: He states that our lands are actually His, too. In fact, He tells us that we *ourselves* belong to Him.

And He's right. He is God, after all.

93

God blesses us for giving to Him.

Honor the LORD *with. . .the firstfruits of all your
increase; so your barns will be filled with plenty.*
PROVERBS 3:9–10

God commanded the Israelites to tithe (give Him 10 percent
of) all their earnings. These tithes were used to support God's
priests and His place of worship and to care for the poor. Tithing
was a way of thanking God for blessing them materially. They
didn't "lose" by giving, either, because God blessed them more as a
result.

Whether you believe Christians today should tithe, or simply
give as they're able, the principle is clear: give to God and He will
give back to you.

94

God blesses *all* giving—great and small.

*He who sows sparingly will also reap sparingly,
and he who sows bountifully will also reap bountifully.*
2 CORINTHIANS 9:6

This simple farming principle also holds true in God's kingdom:
the Lord not only blesses you when you give, but He blesses
you in proportion to how much you give. So if you can afford to
give generously, do so. God gives great dividends! Now, if you only
give a little, well, you'll *still* be blessed. . .just not as greatly.

But remember, if you're going through lean times, the little you
can afford to give counts for more than a millionaire giving a lot.

95

We must keep our promises.

Whoever falsely boasts of giving is like clouds
and wind without rain.
PROVERBS 25:14

Some people are quick to promise that they'll do something—
they pledge to give money to a needy cause or volunteer their
time to help with a project. But then they don't follow through.
They *mean* well, but intentions must translate into deeds—
otherwise it's all clouds and wind but no rain on the thirsty land.

Don't make promises carelessly, and don't break your word
carelessly, either. Carry through on what you say you'll do.

96

God always repays His loans.

He who has pity on the poor lends to the LORD,
and He will pay back what he has given.
PROVERBS 19:17

The Old Testament writers stressed giving to the poor, the
helpless, and the destitute. Jesus constantly repeated this
theme—and the apostles at Jerusalem urged Paul to "remember the
poor" (Galatians 2:10). Remember to help them, that is.

In order to motivate us to give to those who cannot repay us,
Proverbs tells us to think of it as a temporary loan to the Lord.
God will not default on His loans. He will pay back whatever we
give. . .and then some.

97

We should do good deeds.

*Tabitha. . .was full of good works
and charitable deeds which she did.*
ACTS 9:36

Tabitha may not have had much money to give, but she did have a great deal of love, and she gave of her time freely. She was a gifted seamstress and was constantly sewing clothing to give to those who had need.

We all can find ways to do charitable deeds for others. If nothing else, we can offer our hands and our time to help them. Or we can lend a pair of sympathetic ears to the discouraged.

98

Life is often hard for Christians.

*"We must through many tribulations
enter the kingdom of God."*
ACTS 14:22

Some Christians assume that God will so bless believers that no trouble will ever befall them. If the early Christians had entertained such a doctrine, Paul set them straight very quickly. He went from city to city exhorting them to continue in the faith and warning, "We'll endure lots of trials and troubles before we get to heaven." No sugarcoating the message there!

We, too, will face tough times. Let us therefore resolve that, come what may, we, too, will continue to be faithful to God.

99

Hard times won't last forever.

May the God of all grace. . .after you have suffered a while,
perfect, establish, strengthen, and settle you.
1 PETER 5:10

When we're in the middle of suffering, or enduring trouble
that tests our resolve, it's comforting to know that it won't
last forever. God may allow us to suffer for a while, but it's not His
intention that we do so endlessly. God cares for us, and He knows
our limits.

All suffering that God's people endure serves a purpose—a
good purpose, ultimately. And after the trouble is past, God takes us
out of the furnace, settles us, establishes us, and strengthens us.

100

Victory comes to those
who persevere.

Let us not grow weary while doing good, for in
due season we shall reap if we do not lose heart.
GALATIANS 6:9

It's *wise* to let go of futile ventures and move on to productive
things. But too often, we let worthy dreams die because we
become weary with a lack of results and give up.

It can be difficult to know which situation holds true with
personal visions or ventures, but it's never difficult when it comes
to Christian living. We are *never* to stop choosing right over wrong
or doing good to others.

It may take a while, but we will always reap a reward.

101

God gets good out of bad situations.

We know that all things work together
for good to those who love God.
ROMANS 8:28

This verse *isn't* saying that all things that happen to Christians
are good. Some things are detrimental or just plain wrong, and
shouldn't have happened.

But God is loving and powerful, and He is in the business
of redeeming lives and situations. He can make all experiences—
including negative ones—*work together* for His purposes so that
good comes from them in the end.

Not always in this life, but certainly in the next, all tears will be
wiped away and all wrongs righted.

102

God corrects and trains us.

"Behold, happy is the man whom God corrects;
therefore do not despise the chastening of the Almighty."
JOB 5:17

We often like to think we're doing pretty much okay and have
no need of major correction, thank you very much. We're
not happy, therefore, when God sends sickness or complications or
financial reversals into our lives. "O God! Why are you punishing
me?" we cry. (What we often mean is, "Why me?")

Cheer up! It's not punishment. It's God disciplining us. We're
His sons and daughters, and He loves us enough to correct us.
That thought ought to make us happy.

103

We must not give in to despair.

*We are hard-pressed on every side, yet not crushed;
we are perplexed, but not in despair.*
2 CORINTHIANS 4:8

Even the "great" apostle Paul confessed that he felt the stress at times. Pressure was bearing down on him from every side till he felt like he'd be crushed under the strain—but he *wasn't* crushed. And there were days when he was perplexed. He either didn't know why God had allowed something to happen, or he had no idea what he should do—but he didn't give in to despair.

He just kept trusting God and praying till his circumstances changed.

104

We *need* friends and to *be* friends.

*God, who comforts the downcast,
comforted us by the coming of Titus.*
2 CORINTHIANS 7:6

When Paul was in Macedonia, there was trouble all around. He admitted that he felt fear. He was exhausted. Paul could take a lot, but he was only human. He got to where he was downcast, and the Greek word used here means "depressed."

God *Himself* comforts the downcast, but He also uses people. This time He sent Paul's close friend Titus to encourage him. May we be that kind of friend to others, and may we be open to receiving comfort when we're down.

105

Fear is not from God.

God has not given us a spirit of fear,
but of power and of love and of a sound mind.
2 TIMOTHY 1:7

When we become Christians, God's Spirit enters and begins to transform our lives. Now, if we feel gripped by fear, we need to realize that God is not the one giving us that fear. (Fear is not one of the gifts of the Spirit.)

We should reject such fear and overcome it by reminding ourselves that the Holy Spirit gives us *good* and *empowering* gifts like love, power, and a sound mind. Claim these God-given gifts, and they will displace fear.

106

Faith can conquer fear.

"Why are you so fearful?
How is it that you have no faith?"
MARK 4:40

When you're nearly overwhelmed by troubles or danger, there seems to be good reason to fear. The twelve disciples in the storm-tossed, wave-washed boat certainly thought so!

What Jesus asked was not, "Why are you afraid *at all*?" but, "Why are you *so full of fear*?" The boat was still bearing up, but their minds were already swamped and sinking—to the point where they had no faith left.

It may require a terrific effort of will, but we must face and overcome fear with faith.

107

Love kicks fear out the door.

There is no fear in love; but perfect love casts out fear. . .
he who fears has not been made perfect in love.
1 JOHN 4:18

Most of us understand how faith can overcome fear. After all, faith is a powerful force, the opposite of fear—which results from a *lack* of faith. But how, we ask, can something as "sweet and gentle" as *love* thrust out fear?

Well, God *is* love and God is all-powerful. He is the Light that pushes back the darkness. A person who is "perfect in love" is so full of God's Spirit that there's little room left for darkness, doubt, and fear.

108

Trust helps you sleep.

When you lie down, you will not be afraid;
yes, you will lie down and your sleep will be sweet.
PROVERBS 3:24

Perhaps when you lie down at night you can barely fall asleep. You're not afraid of a monster under your bed—haven't been for years. You're not living in a war-wracked city, either. So what has you afraid? Bills, your kids, your marriage, the economy, the future. . . Call it worry, but if it's stressing you so badly you can't sleep, it's fear.

God wants you to be well rested. So pray—hand your problems off to God and trust Him to take care of things. Then have sweet dreams.

109

We must resist the devil.

Submit to God. Resist the devil and he will flee from you.
Draw near to God and He will draw near to you.
JAMES 4:7–8

Resisting the devil involves more than just commanding him in Jesus' name to leave—though that's certainly a necessary step. The key to resisting Satan is found in the two other admonitions: "draw near to God" and "submit to God."

When we're close to God we experience more of His power. When we submit to God's will instead of resisting Him, the devil no longer has a toehold.

Kneeling before God enables us to stand up to Satan. And he *will* flee.

110

God's Word helps us overcome evil.

The word of God abides in you,
and you have overcome the wicked one.
1 JOHN 2:14

When Jesus was fasting and the devil repeatedly tried to tempt Him to sin, Jesus quoted the Word of God to refute him. Again and again, Jesus replied, "It is written. . ." then quoted a passage that exposed the devil's lie. We need to do the same.

That's where it really pays to know what the Bible says.

Of course, we need to *obey* those verses, not merely memorize them like lines from a theatrical production. Then we can speak the Word of God with authority.

111

Satan constantly fights God's will.

We wanted to come to you—even I, Paul,
time and again—but Satan hindered us.
1 THESSALONIANS 2:18

Have you ever tried to do something for God and found yourself fighting through delays and roadblocks every foot of the way? "Why?" you ask.

This happened to the apostle Paul, too. Satan constantly fights God's will. (No surprise there.)

Again and again, the devil hindered Paul from visiting the Christians in Thessalonica. Satan wanted to stop him, or if nothing else, to slow him down.

If that happens to you, don't give up. Pray for God to drive off the devil and push on through.

112

Spending time with God gives us strength.

But those who wait on the LORD shall renew their strength.
ISAIAH 40:31

Everyone runs out of strength at some point. Even youths with seemingly boundless physical energy eventually stop bounding. And all of us reach points where our mental stamina wears out and our spiritual power flickers.

How do we renew our mental and spiritual strength? By spending time with God and allowing Him to recharge our batteries. It takes a while, we have to wait on Him, but if we want to keep going, we have to set aside that time.

It is *so* worth it!

113

God upholds the fallen.

Though he fall, he shall not be utterly cast down;
for the LORD upholds him with His hand.
PSALM 37:24

You've seen that man or woman: They're struggling in hard times. They're battered this way and that till they weaken. . .and then they fall. They're worn out, or some temptation takes them down. Perhaps you've been there yourself.

But somehow they get back up. They've been cast down but not utterly cast down, because something caught them. That something was the Lord. Never forget that "underneath are the everlasting arms" (Deuteronomy 33:27).

God's mighty hand upholds the fallen and enables them to rise again.

114

Happiness strengthens us.

"Do not sorrow, for the joy of the LORD is your strength."
NEHEMIAH 8:10

It's right to mourn and weep when we realize how far we've strayed and disobeyed God. That's what the Jews in Nehemiah's day did. But there's also a time to receive His forgiveness and rejoice. It's not God's will for us to flagellate ourselves, to continually mope around discouraged and defeated.

Yes, God has forgiven our sins! Yes, He still loves us! Yes, He gives us fresh mercy! Knowing these things should give us joy. That joy then gives us strength to face life.

115

Jesus has power to heal.

Jesus went about. . .healing all kinds of sickness
and all kinds of disease among the people.
MATTHEW 4:23

While He was on earth, Jesus was constantly healing
sicknesses and diseases. From morning till evening, the sick
came to Him, and Jesus healed them all. It was a clear way to show
that He *loved* them. It was also proof that He was the Son of God.

Thank God for good doctors and effective medicines these days.
They help many people. But Jesus *still* loves us, and He's *still* the Son
of God and *still* has the power to heal—so don't forget to pray.

116

Being sick is sometimes
a good thing.

It is good for me that I have been afflicted,
that I may learn Your statutes.
PSALM 119:71

If Jesus can heal, why, we ask, doesn't He always heal us when
we're sick? Well, perhaps we don't have the faith that He can do
the miracle. But there's also another reason. . . .

Sometimes it's actually good for us to have a handicap or suffer
sickness. Paul had to have a "thorn in the flesh" (apparently an
eye disease) to keep him humble. Other times, God allows us to
become sick to get our attention and speak to us about things we've
been ignoring.

117

God helps the desperate
and the distressed.

*You have been a strength to the poor, a strength to the needy in his
distress, a refuge from the storm.*
ISAIAH 25:4

When we're passing through a dark valley, we often feel
abandoned by God: We cry out to Him but hear no answer.
We weep that we can't bear up under the strain and beg Him
to deliver us. . .but no answer. We pray for protection from the
tempest. . .but still no answer.

And yet we pass through our deep distress. We realize that
God has, after all, given us the strength to carry our load. The
storm passes and we are still standing.

118

God delivers those
who trust Him.

*He shall deliver them from the wicked,
and save them, because they trust in Him.*
PSALM 37:40

There may come a time in your life when a truly wicked person
determines to bring you to ruin—and there may seem to be
little you can do to stop him or her. What do you do? What *can*
you do?

You must pray to God to save you. And no matter how grim or
threatening the circumstances seem, you must never stop trusting
that God has the *power* to protect you, and that He *will* protect
you. And He will.

119

God disposes of the wicked.

*God will rebuke them and they will flee far away. . .
like a rolling thing before the whirlwind.*
ISAIAH 17:13

Your enemies may be rooted in secure positions of power, but God is far, far more powerful. He can suddenly rise up in His fury like a windstorm in the desert, tear the wicked up by the roots, and send them rolling and bouncing powerlessly along. He thrusts them along like tumbleweed. . .till they are gone.

Living through a desert storm is an awe-inspiring experience, but more terrifying still is to see God rebuke the wicked with the force of a whirlwind.

120

God foils the crafty.

*"He frustrates the devices of the crafty,
so that their hands cannot carry out their plans."*
JOB 5:12

Prayer moves the hand of God, and in a world increasingly filled with con artists, hackers, and identity thieves, we certainly need to pray for God's protection. Those who wish to defraud us think they're so clever, but God is even cleverer. He can stymie their efforts and cause everything to go so haywire that they can't carry out their plans. They won't even be able to set a mousetrap properly.

We can't confound and confuse the crafty like that, but we *can* pray.

121

God's angels protect us.

He shall give His angels charge over you,
to keep you in all your ways.
PSALM 91:11

Many people believe that God assigns a guardian angel to
protect us from the day we're born till the day we die. Some
insist that we have *two* angels constantly guarding us, one on each
hand. The Bible doesn't tell us the details, but we can be sure of this:
angels *do* watch over us.

God gives them charge over us. To be "given charge" doesn't
mean that they boss us around; it means that they're commanded to
watch out for us.

That's a comforting thought.

122

God protects us every day.

Through the LORD's mercies we are not consumed, because His
compassions fail not. They are new every morning.
LAMENTATIONS 3:22–23

So many things can go wrong every day, and we are like toddlers,
almost daily stumbling between hot stoves and medicine
cabinets. Accidents and troubles would surely swallow us up if it
weren't for the Lord's mercy. His compassion just never peters out.

This isn't to say that God protects us from all harm or shields
us from every consequence of our carelessness—but the fact that
we're still here is proof that He hasn't allowed them to *consume* us.

123

God can do absolutely anything.

"Behold, I am the LORD, the God of all flesh.
Is there anything too hard for Me?"
JEREMIAH 32:27

That is the question, isn't it? And the answer, in the same chapter, is, "You have made the heavens and the earth by Your great power. . . .There is nothing too hard for you" (Jeremiah 32:17).

God not only created all life on earth, but the earth itself. In fact, He made the entire universe of which the earth is a very small part. A God with *that* much power would hardly find our problems too difficult.

We need to remind ourselves of that occasionally.

124

God can do what we can't.

"With men this is impossible,
but with God all things are possible."
MATTHEW 19:26

When problems come our way, our first reaction is usually to try to solve it—which is a good thing. God has given us problem-solving brains for that very purpose. But some problems are simply too difficult to resolve. Even bringing in the experts won't help.

It's frustrating to realize that we're in an impossible situation, but fortunately, there's a miracle worker who can help us—God. He has unlimited power. He can do literally anything.

So don't wait too long before you call Him.

125

God makes weak people strong.

When I am weak, then I am strong.
2 CORINTHIANS 12:10

Jesus taught many conundrums that turn conventional human wisdom on its head: "The first shall be last. . . . Bless those who curse you. . . . He that loses his life saves it. . . .The weak are strong." Odd statements. . .yet, amazingly, they *work*.

The reason these "upside-down" principles work is because they factor God into the equation. When we're weak and trusting, God's power rests on us. That makes us strong—*far* stronger than we'd be if we depended only on our strength.

126

God doesn't need big armies.

*"Nothing restrains the LORD from saving
by many or by few."*
1 SAMUEL 14:6

When God parted the Red Sea and defeated the Egyptians, He didn't need any help. Moses basically said, "Stand back and watch God save us!" (Exodus 14:13).

Yet when God says that He *does* want people involved, we suddenly get the idea that He needs a *lot* of us—a regular army, in fact. Not so. God might use many people to save the day, or He might use only a few.

Never forget that though God is *one*, He counts for "many."

127

We should witness to others.

*"Go into all the world and preach
the gospel to every creature."*
MARK 16:15

When Jesus gave this command two thousand years ago,
Christians headed out, preaching the Gospel. They were
not only living examples of what a follower of Christ should be,
but they spoke up and *told* others about Jesus.

This command didn't just apply to the apostles who heard Jesus
say it—all Christians back then preached the Gospel. And it's not
only for pastors and evangelists today—it's for all of us.

The world still needs to hear about Jesus, so let's tell them!

128

There's no need to
be ashamed of Jesus.

*I am not ashamed of the gospel of Christ, for it is the power of God to
salvation for everyone who believes.*
ROMANS 1:16

Many of us genuinely love Jesus, understand that only He can
save us, yet we don't talk to others about Him. We say that
we're shy. We're ashamed of being labeled a religious nut. We don't
like being preachy or pushy.

So let's *not* be pushy or preachy. And if we speak gently and
not wild eyed, we'll avoid being labeled a fanatic. We must believe
that people *need* salvation then pray for God to make opportunities
for us to speak to them. . .gently.

129

We must know what we believe.

*Always be ready to give a defense to everyone
who asks you a reason for the hope that is in you.*
1 PETER 3:15

Some people, when they learn that you're a Christian, will ask *why* you believe there's a God, why you have faith in Jesus, why you have hope of eternal life, etc. Whether they're asking sincerely or skeptically, you must be prepared to give them a reason why you believe.

You don't have to give complicated answers, but you should know your Bible well enough to give an intelligent answer with sincerity. It also helps to read books that explain and defend the Christian faith.

130

You're bound to have enemies.

*All who desire to live godly in
Christ Jesus will suffer persecution.*
2 TIMOTHY 3:12

It seems like many Christians go through their entire lives without ever experiencing persecution, but persecution doesn't just mean being beaten or driven from town—as happens in some countries. It also means being lied about, maligned, and opposed.

Many a peaceful Christian who has taken a stand for godly values and resisted pressure to back down has been surprised at how suddenly persecution can arise—even from former friends.

Don't be surprised. Jesus was persecuted, and we will be, too, if we follow Him.

131

Be *glad* if you're persecuted.

"Blessed are you when they revile and
persecute you. . .for My sake."
MATTHEW 5:11

When you obey Jesus' commands and do what's right, and foul-mouthed people revile (curse) you for it, the experience can be unpleasant and embarrassing. . .even intimidating. Of course, that's the effect they're trying to achieve.

But don't let it get to you. Jesus says you're blessed when people curse you and treat you badly. You're so blessed, in fact, that you should rejoice! Why? Because God will richly compensate you in heaven for everything you suffer for His sake.

That's a promise!

132

We *can* endure hostility.

Consider Him who endured such hostility from sinners against Himself,
lest you become weary and discouraged in your souls.
HEBREWS 12:3

Knowing that you'll be rewarded in heaven for suffering persecution here on earth is a great encouragement. However, if the opposition goes on and on, even promises of heavenly rewards can seem distant. So how do you endure prolonged hostility without becoming discouraged?

Look to Jesus. Consider how much God's own Son suffered—*years* of hostile opposition from His enemies, lies, attacks on His reputation—and finally beatings, mockery, and crucifixion.

You haven't suffered that much, so take heart.

133

We can defeat ignorant, foolish men.

*This is the will of God, that by doing good you may
put to silence the ignorance of foolish men.*
1 PETER 2:15

Many people today have skewed, unfavorable opinions about
Christianity. Some have had unpleasant encounters with
Christians, true, but many get their views from biased media
reports or the constant disparaging remarks made by vocal
unbelievers. The Bible calls this "the ignorance of foolish men."

God also tells us how to *dispel* this ignorance: we are to live
exemplary lives, be honest in business, obey the law, and do good.
If we do this consistently, people will eventually realize that
Christianity is a good thing.

134

We must remember persecuted Christians.

*Remember the prisoners as if chained with them—those who
are mistreated—since you yourselves are in the body also.*
HEBREWS 13:3

In America, we usually don't suffer serious persecution for our
faith, but Christians in many nations suffer terribly. They're
mistreated, attacked, imprisoned, tortured, and killed. We must not
become so settled in our good life—or absorbed by our problems—
that we forget them. We must feel their pain as if chained right
beside them.

If we can help persecuted Christians, we should. Many
churches even sponsor suffering believers as refugees.

Most of all, however, we must remember them in prayer.

135

Judgment is slow for a reason.

"You are a gracious and merciful God,
slow to anger and abundant in lovingkindness,
One who relents from doing harm."
JONAH 4:2

When people threaten us, we wonder, "What's God waiting for? Why doesn't He judge them. . .*now?*" Jonah wondered that same thing. The Assyrians were militaristic, oppressive, and cruel, yet just when God was poised to destroy their capital, Nineveh, they repented. So God postponed judgment.

A very frustrated Jonah knew why: God loved the Assyrians, and He longed to show even them mercy. Fortunately for the people of the world, God is more merciful than we are.

136

God doesn't go by our schedule.

"Though it tarries, wait for it; because it
will surely come, it will not tarry."
HABAKKUK 2:3

God has made many promises in His Word—promises to bless us if we obey Him, and to answer our prayers. Yet many times it appears that God isn't doing anything. . .and we despair.

We're so impatient. We expect God's train to come in on our schedule, and when it doesn't, we think He's late. We don't want to wait one more moment. Yet, if God takes a little longer than we'd anticipated, it does us good to continue to trust and to wait. The time will come when God *will* act.

137

It's worth waiting for God.

My soul waits for the Lord more than
those who watch for the morning.
PSALM 130:6

In ancient days, soldiers stood atop city walls by night on guard duty. They were cold and had to be constantly vigilant, so they longed for sunrise when the danger was past and their shift ended.

When we spend long months praying and waiting, and God finally answers, it's like the sun rising over the dark hills. We knew that God *would* eventually answer. It just took time for the day to arrive.

Keep on watching and waiting no matter how dark it is. Sunrise is coming!

138

God can be trusted completely.

Trust in the LORD with all your heart,
and lean not on your own understanding.
PROVERBS 3:5

God's ways are so much higher than our ways. We're like children learning basic addition and subtraction, compared to a college professor teaching advanced formulas that fill entire blackboards. Yet we insist that all life should be as simple as 1 + 1 = 2.

We can't possibly understand how God's ways work or how He gets the results that He does. We're way out of our depth. We just have to place our hand in His, trust that He knows what He's doing, and obey Him.

139

Give God *all* your worries.

Casting all your care upon Him, for He cares for you.
1 PETER 5:7

When Peter says "care" he means anxious thoughts. Some of us worry about every little thing. Others of us don't sweat the small stuff; no, we only get frantic about middle-sized problems and big problems.

But whatever problems arise to harass us, the Bible tells us to heave them into God's hands. They'll just wear us down and wear us out if we try to carry them.

We can trust God to bear our concerns. After all, He loves us. He cares for us.

140

God removes our anxiety.

Be anxious for nothing, but. . .
let your requests be made known to God.
PHILIPPIANS 4:6

When Paul says, "Be anxious for nothing," it's understood that there *are* situations that you should be concerned about. The question is what you do about them. Do you just think and think about them until your mind's spinning like a hamster on a treadmill? Or do you turn that concern into a prayer and ask God to help you?

If you earnestly pray, the Lord will answer. Then He promises, "the peace of God. . .will guard your hearts and minds" (verse 7).

141

God wants us to have fun.

A feast is made for laughter.
ECCLESIASTES 10:19

While we must take our faith seriously, there are times when we need to lighten up and have a good laugh. A family feast where we enjoy good food and good company is literally *made* for laughter. And so were we.

When the prodigal son returned, his overjoyed father threw a party, and everyone enjoyed the festivities. Only the overly serious older brother was angry at the "waste" and refused to join in.

Remember: God wants us to enjoy family, friends, food, and fun!

142

It's healthy to be happy.

A merry heart does good, like medicine.
PROVERBS 17:22

People have known for thousands of years that being happy and laughing was a good thing. It didn't take a lot of thought to come to that conclusion. But the Bible took it a step further, stating that merriment literally had the power to heal just like medicine.

Sure enough, in recent years clinical tests have shown that laughter reduces stress hormones, increases pain tolerance, strengthens the immune system, and increases the level of health-enhancing endorphins. All good stuff.

143

We can be happy in hard times.

You greatly rejoice, though now for a little while,
if need be, you have been grieved by various trials.
1 PETER 1:6

Perhaps you're thinking, "I'd like to be happy, but I'm really going through a rough time now." Sorrow is the right reaction at times, and is actually necessary, but it's possible to sorrow too deep and too long. We can become "swallowed up with too much sorrow" (2 Corinthians 2:7). We must remember to rejoice.

Think of the joy you'll one day enjoy, eternally, in heaven. Really *believe* that it will happen one day, and you can't help but rejoice in the midst of your grieving.

144

This world will end.

Behold, He is coming with clouds. . .and all the
tribes of the earth will mourn because of Him.
REVELATION 1:7

Jesus is coming again just as He promised He would! And when He returns, the world as we now know it will come to an end. It will not be a happy day for the unsaved who've been persecuting Christians. They'll mourn when they see Jesus because they'll realize that we were telling them the truth. . .only now it's too late.

It will be a very *happy* day for Christians, however. The day man's rule over this world ends, heaven on earth begins.

145

We'll be transformed at the Rapture.

We also eagerly wait for the Savior, the Lord Jesus Christ,
who will transform our lowly body.
PHILIPPIANS 3:20–21

We long for Jesus to come back. Not only will He end all wars, bring justice on earth, feed the hungry, and restore the world to its original paradisiacal state. . .but He will miraculously transform our physical bodies.

No longer will we be weak, sick, aging, and mortal. We will be powerful, glorious, forever young, and immortal! We will be completely changed—with no more pain, suffering, and disease. . . ever again.

No wonder we eagerly await Jesus' Second Coming!

146

Jesus will judge Christians.

We must all appear before the judgment seat of Christ,
that each one may receive the things done in the body.
2 CORINTHIANS 5:10

One day, all Christians will appear before Jesus to account for what they have done with their lives. But the Judgment Seat of Christ is different from the judgment of the world when the wicked are condemned. Those who appear before Christ at this time are saved.

It will be a time of great rejoicing as Jesus richly rewards Christians for every good deed they have done, every loving word they have ever spoken, and every bit of suffering they endured for His name.

147

Bad deeds will be burned up.

If anyone's work is burned, he will suffer loss;
but he himself will be saved, yet so as through fire.
1 CORINTHIANS 3:15

Jesus will reward Christians for the good they've done. . .but
what about their *bad* deeds—their selfish attitudes, the time
wasted, their sins? Jesus took the punishment for sin on the cross,
so we know that's taken care of.

All of their bad deeds will be utterly burned up. They
themselves will be saved, but will "suffer loss" because they'll
receive no reward for those wasted portions of their life.

Only their good works will enter with them into eternity.

148

Happy days are coming to stay.

"God will wipe away every tear from their eyes;
there shall be no more death, nor sorrow, nor crying."
REVELATION 21:4

Many Christians believe that when we realize the ways we
failed to live for Christ, we'll weep. . .that these are the tears
that God will wipe away. That's part of it.

But there's a deeper meaning here: we try our best to live for
Christ in this world but are often beset by sickness, financial lack,
the death of loved ones, suffering, and persecution for Jesus' sake. All
these sad things will one day end.

We'll weep no longer in heaven—just enjoy endless happiness.

149

You'll have your day in the sun.

*"Then the righteous will shine forth as
the sun in the kingdom of their Father."*
MATTHEW 13:43

Jesus said that the poor and the meek (the humble) are blessed, for they shall inherit the kingdom of heaven (Matthew 5:3, 5). They don't *seem* too blessed at the moment: they're weak, and the mighty of this world overlook them and tread them underfoot. But the day is coming when the righteous will reign with Christ, and *no one* will be able to overlook them.

When God's kingdom comes, and He rewards those who love Him, they'll blaze with glory like the sun!

150

Heaven is unimaginably wonderful.

*"Eye has not seen, nor ear heard, nor have entered into the heart of man,
the things which God has prepared for those who love Him."*
1 CORINTHIANS 2:9

Paul penned this line in AD 55 and at the time, Christians had very little idea what heaven was like, or how wonderful it was. Certainly no one had been there and returned to write about it in any detail—not till AD 95, that is, when John was transported into the heavenlies and wrote the book of Revelation.

Of course, not even John's breathtaking description truly does heaven justice. As the saying goes, "You had to have *been* there!"

One day you *will* be there.

199 Bible People,
Places, and Things

Jean Fischer

CONTENTS

INTRODUCTION

The Bible is a big book—actually, a collection of books. Under one cover, you'll find 66 separate books, totaling 1,189 chapters and hundreds of thousands of words. You know the Bible's important, but it can be a bit daunting. That's why we created *199 Bible People, Places, and Things.*

In this little book, you'll find brief, easy-to-read definitions or descriptions of some of the most important names and words in scripture. From Aaron and Abraham through Yahweh, Worship, and Zacchaeus, here are the basic details to help you understand each one. And, if you'd like to study further, we've included plenty of Bible references.

We hope you enjoy this brief survey of 199 of the Bible's most important words and names. As you get to know your Bible better, you'll also gain understanding of the great God who gave you the Bible—the God who made you, keeps you, and offers you salvation.

1. AARON

MOSES' OLDER BROTHER. Moses wasn't a good speaker, so God told Aaron to speak for him. Moses was the leader and Aaron his spokesman. Aaron helped Moses lead the Hebrew slaves out of Egypt (Exodus 7–12), and God chose Aaron to be Israel's first high priest. He wasn't perfect: when the people asked him to make a statue of a god they could worship, Aaron agreed and fashioned a golden calf (Exodus 32:1–4). God forgave Aaron after Moses prayed for him. Neither Aaron nor Moses made it to the Promised Land because they disobeyed God at a place called Meribah. They were supposed to speak to a rock to create miracle water in the desert—but Moses was angry with the people and hit the rock with a stick instead (Numbers 20:6–12).

2. ABRAHAM

A MAN OF GREAT FAITH. Abraham and his wife, Sarah, had a son named Isaac, for whom they'd waited for years. But when God decided to test Abraham's faith, He asked the old man to offer Isaac as a sacrifice (Genesis 22:1–13). Abraham was about to do what God asked when the angel of the LORD appeared, saying, "Don't hurt the boy!" (Genesis 22:12 CEV). God had evidence that Abraham would do anything for Him, and the Lord provided another sacrifice—a ram caught in a bush. The apostle Paul called Abraham "the father of us all" (Romans 4:16), the people who come to God through faith in Jesus Christ.

3. ADAM

THE FIRST PERSON ON EARTH. Adam was good and intelligent (Genesis 2:19–20), but he wasn't perfect—because he disobeyed God's one rule and ate the fruit of a tree God had said to stay away from. Adam was the first worker (Genesis 2:8, 15) and the first husband. God made a woman named Eve to be Adam's wife (Genesis 2:18–25). Their home was the Garden of Eden, but when Adam and Eve sinned, God sent them away from their perfect home forever (Genesis 3:22–24).

4. ADOPTION

TO TAKE SOMEONE INTO YOUR FAMILY AND MAKE THEM YOUR OWN. Children are not always born into the family they grow up in. Instead, they are chosen by nonbiological parents who love them. The apostle Paul talked about a spiritual adoption (Romans 11:1–32; Galatians 4:4–7), saying that anyone can be adopted as God's child if he or she has faith in Jesus Christ (Galatians 3:24–26).

5. ADVOCATE

A PERSON WHO SUPPORTS SOMEONE OR SOMETHING. People who speak up or do something for a cause they believe in are called advocates. In many ways, an advocate is a helper. The Bible says that Jesus is our Advocate: "If you. . .sin, Jesus Christ always does the right thing, and he will speak to the Father for us" (1 John 2:1 CEV).

6. Alpha and Omega

A TERM THAT MEANS THE BEGINNING AND THE ENDING. In the Greek alphabet, Alpha is the first letter and Omega the last. They remind us that God the Father, His Son Jesus, and the Holy Spirit are here forever and ever. Jesus promised that when He said, "I am the Alpha and the Omega, the Beginning and the End. . .who is and who was and who is to come, the Almighty" (Revelation 1:8 NKJV).

7. Andrew

ONE OF JESUS' DISCIPLES, ALSO PETER'S BROTHER. Andrew was a fisherman from the town of Bethsaida (John 1:44). He was a follower of John the Baptist (John 1:35–40), and he introduced Peter to Jesus (John 1:41–42). Andrew was the disciple who brought to Jesus a boy with five loaves of bread and two fishes. Jesus used that small lunch to feed more than five thousand people (John 6:1–14).

8. Angel of the Lord

A SPECIAL ANGEL WHO SERVES AS GOD'S SPOKESMAN. He was around a lot in Old Testament times: He appeared to Abraham when he was about to sacrifice his son Isaac (Genesis 22:12), to Hagar in the wilderness (Genesis 16:7–12), and to Moses in the burning bush (Exodus 3:2–3). He also appeared to Gideon (Judges 6:11–12), Balaam (Numbers 22:21–35), Elijah (2 Kings 1:3), David (1 Chronicles 21:16), and others.

9. Antichrist

SOMEONE WHO IS AGAINST JESUS. Many believe an antichrist will appear at the end of time as the enemy of Christ and all Christians. Another name for this antichrist is the beast (Revelation 13). He will say that Jesus is not the Christ (1 John 2:22–23) and boastfully go against everything holy. He will even sit on God's throne and pretend to be God (2 Thessalonians 2:3–4). In the end, the antichrist will die: "The Lord Jesus will kill him simply by breathing on him" (2 Thessalonians 2:8 CEV).

10. Ark of the Covenant

A GOLD-PLATED WOODEN CHEST CONTAINING THE TEN COMMANDMENTS. The Ten Commandments were carved on two stone tablets (Exodus 34:28; Deuteronomy 10:3–4), and God said to put them into the ark of the covenant. The New Testament book of Hebrews talks about some manna and Aaron's rod also being in the ark (9:4). God wanted the manna to be placed before the ark (Exodus 16:32–34) to remind the people that He took care of them in the wilderness. Aaron's rod was a sign to those who rebelled against the Lord (Numbers 17:10). God gave detailed instructions for making the ark (Exodus 25:10–22), and when it was done, it was a holy symbol, showing that God was with His people (Exodus 25:22). At first, the ark was stored in the tabernacle (Exodus 26:33). When the Israelites foolishly took it into battle (1 Samuel 4:1–5), the Philistines captured it (1 Samuel 4:10–11). The Philistines were afflicted while they had the ark, and returned it—later, it was kept in the temple in Jerusalem (1 Kings 8:1–9). King Nebuchadnezzar of Babylon might have stolen it from there (2 Chronicles 36:7, 18), though no one knows for sure what happened to it.

11. ASCENSION OF CHRIST

JESUS' RETURN TO HEAVEN AFTER HE ROSE FROM THE DEAD. Jesus was crucified, then buried in a tomb. Three days later, He came to life again and stayed on earth for forty days (Luke 24:1–49; Acts 1:3). After that, He ascended into heaven to be with God (Luke 24:50–51). Jesus' ascension happened at the Mount of Olives, and His disciples were there to see it. "While they were watching, he was taken up into a cloud. They could not see him, but as he went up, they kept looking up into the sky. Suddenly two men dressed in white clothes were standing there beside them. They said, 'Why are you men from Galilee standing here and looking up into the sky? Jesus has been taken to heaven. But he will come back in the same way that you have seen him go'" (Acts 1:9–11 CEV).

12. ATONEMENT

SETTLING DIFFERENCES BETWEEN GOD AND MAN THROUGH A SACRIFICE. In Old Testament times, *atonement* required making animal sacrifices to God. But when Jesus died on the cross, He became the ultimate sacrifice to God. He died so that everyone who believed in Him could be forgiven for their sins (2 Corinthians 5:21). Christ's atonement—the work He did on the cross—is our foundation for peace (Ephesians 2:13–16).

13. BAAL

THE PRIMARY (FALSE) GOD OF THE CANAANITES. They believed Baal made crops grow and livestock reproduce. Sadly, some of God's people worshipped Baal, too, breaking the second commandment (Exodus 20:4–5). God sent His prophet Elijah to prove there was only one true God, in a dramatic encounter on Mount Carmel. Many of the people turned from their evil ways, but the rest of them were killed. Read the whole story in 1 Kings 18:1–40.

14. BAPTISM

A CHRISTIAN CEREMONY OF FAITH WHERE PEOPLE ARE DIPPED IN WATER, OR WATER IS POURED OR SPRINKLED ON THEIR HEADS. The ceremony shows our faith in Jesus Christ publicly, and is a symbol of the washing away of our sins. *Baptize* comes from the Greek word *baptizo*, meaning to dunk, dip, or plunge. The New Testament character John the Baptist baptized many people, including Jesus (Matthew 3:4–17). Since Jesus had no sin, He didn't need to be baptized—but He did it to set an example for us (Matthew 3:15).

15. BARABBAS

A NOTORIOUS CRIMINAL. Barabbas was already in jail when Jesus was arrested, imprisoned for sedition and murder. When Jesus was brought to Pontius Pilate, the Roman governor of Judea, to be judged, a mob began shouting for the release of Barabbas. Pilate gave in to their demand: Barabbas was set free, and Jesus was sent to be crucified (Mark 15:6–15).

16. Barnabas

A FRIEND AND COWORKER OF THE APOSTLE PAUL. **Barnabas's** real name was Joses, but the apostles called him *Barnabas*, meaning "one who encourages others" (Acts 4:36 CEV). It was Barnabas who convinced the disciples that Paul—once a violent persecutor of Christians—had truly met Jesus on the road to Damascus. In time, Paul became one of Christianity's greatest influences, making multiple missionary journeys and writing a large portion of the New Testament.

17. Bathsheba

S OLOMON'S MOTHER. King David saw Bathsheba bathing outdoors, and thought she was beautiful. But she was also married—to Uriah, a soldier in David's army. David called her to his palace, slept with her, and got her pregnant. Then he compounded his sin by making sure that Uriah was killed fighting in a battle (2 Samuel 11:14–17). Once Uriah was dead, David married Bathsheba, who ultimately bore him four sons. One of them was Solomon (2 Samuel 12:24), David's successor as king of Israel.

18. BEATITUDES

BLESSINGS. When Jesus gave the Sermon on the Mount, He blessed the people, in statements now called the Beatitudes. Jesus said, "Blessed are the poor in spirit, for theirs is the kingdom of heaven. Blessed are those who mourn, for they will be comforted. Blessed are the meek, for they will inherit the earth. Blessed are those who hunger and thirst for righteousness, for they will be filled. Blessed are the merciful, for they will be shown mercy. Blessed are the pure in heart, for they will see God. Blessed are the peacemakers, for they will be called children of God. Blessed are those who are persecuted because of righteousness, for theirs is the kingdom of heaven. Blessed are you when people insult you, persecute you and falsely say all kinds of evil against you because of me. Rejoice and be glad, because great is your reward in heaven" (Matthew 5:3–12 NIV).

19. BENJAMIN

JOSEPH'S LITTLE BROTHER, THE YOUNGEST OF TWELVE BROTHERS. Their father was Jacob, and Benjamin and Joseph were Dad's favorites (Genesis 37:3; 42:38) because they were the sons of Rachel, the wife Jacob loved the most (Genesis 29:30; 35:24). Benjamin's brothers were jealous of Joseph, so they sold him as a slave to merchants who carried him to Egypt (Genesis 37:28). Years later, Joseph saw his brothers again, and he forgave them. He was especially happy to see his baby brother, Benjamin. A tribe of Israel descended from Benjamin, known as the Benjamites (Judges 20:35).

20. BETHANY

A VILLAGE AT THE FOOT OF THE MOUNT OF OLIVES (MARK 11:1) NEAR JERUSALEM. Jesus went to Bethany often. His good friends Mary, Martha, and Lazarus lived there (John 11:1), and it was in Bethany that Jesus brought Lazarus back to life after he had been dead for four days (John 11:17–44). After Jesus Himself died and came back to life, He ascended into heaven from Bethany (Luke 24:50–51).

21. BETHLEHEM

THE PLACE WHERE JESUS WAS BORN. Jesus' earthly parents, Mary and Joseph, were from Nazareth—but they traveled to Bethlehem for a census since that was Joseph's ancestral hometown. When they arrived, Jesus was born (Luke 2:1–11). Bethlehem is also where King David grew up (1 Samuel 16:1–13), and is sometimes called "the city of David" (Luke 2:4).

22. BIRTHRIGHT

WEALTH FOR AN OLDEST SON. In Bible times, the oldest son was often given many good things. For example, he would get a double share of everything his father owned when his dad died (Deuteronomy 21:17). Then he would take over as the leader of the family. If the son behaved badly, though, his birthright could be taken away. One son who didn't respect his birthright was Esau, who sold the valuable blessing to his younger brother, Jacob, for a single bowl of stew (Genesis 25:29–34)!

23. Blood

THE LIFE-SUSTAINING FLUID OF THE BODY. In Old Testament times, when a person sinned, he killed a healthy, unblemished animal as a sacrifice. The animal's blood was a symbol of the person's blood, or life (Leviticus 17:11). The person didn't have to die for that sin, because the animal took his place. In New Testament times, Jesus sacrificed His own blood and life to pay for *our* sins (Hebrews 9:14). Jesus is sometimes called the "Lamb of God," since He was a perfect sacrifice in every way (1 Peter 1:18–19). Today, when people take communion, they remember that Jesus gave His blood and His life so that God would forgive us for our sins (1 Corinthians 11:25).

24. Body of Christ

ANOTHER NAME FOR CHRIST'S CHURCH. The apostle Paul called the church Christ's body (Colossians 1:24). Jesus' Spirit is always in His body, the church. He rules over it, and is the head of everything in it (Ephesians 1:22–23). Every true believer in any church anywhere in the world is a member of the body of Christ. The Bible says that the members of the body of Christ should help and care for one another (1 Corinthians 12:25–27).

25. Book of the Law

THE LAW ACCORDING TO MOSES. "The Book of the Law" is a name for the first five books of the Old Testament—Genesis, Exodus, Leviticus, Numbers, and Deuteronomy—also called the *Pentateuch*. God gave these laws to Moses, who wrote them down. Then Moses gave them to the priests, who read the laws to the people (Deuteronomy 31:9–11).

26. Brass Serpent

A METAL SNAKE GOD USED TO HEAL PEOPLE BITTEN BY REAL SNAKES. Some of the Israelites became so disrespectful of God that He sent poisonous snakes to bite them (Numbers 21:4–6). The people begged Moses for help, and God told Moses to make a snake out of brass and put it on top of a pole. Anyone who was bitten should look at the snake and they would be healed (Numbers 21:7–9). Jesus compared Himself to the brass serpent in John 3:14–15.

27. Burnt Offering

A GIFT FOR GOD. In Old Testament days, people killed a healthy, unblemished animal, then put parts of the dead animal—its fat, the lower part of its liver, and its two kidneys—on an altar. These parts were burned in a holy ceremony before God (Leviticus 7:1–8).

28. CAIN

THE OLDEST SON OF ADAM AND EVE. Cain was jealous because his younger brother Abel's offerings pleased God. Apparently, Cain didn't give the Lord what He really wanted. Before long, Cain's jealousy led to anger, and he took Abel out into a field and killed him. God punished Cain by sending him away (Genesis 4:3–11), making him a "restless wanderer on the earth" (Genesis 4:12 NIV).

29. CALVARY

THE HILL WHERE JESUS WAS CRUCIFIED (JOHN 19:16–17). The word *Calvary* comes from a Latin word that means "skull." That is why Calvary is sometimes called "the Skull." It's also called "Golgotha" (Mark 15:22). The hill was just outside the city walls of ancient Jerusalem (Luke 23:33). If you go to Jerusalem today, you can visit the place where some say Jesus was crucified. The Church of the Holy Sepulchre marks the site.

30. CANAAN

THE PROMISED LAND. Canaan was mainly between the Mediterranean Sea and the Jordan River. Today, this area is Israel, the West Bank, the Gaza Strip, and parts of Lebanon and Syria. Canaan was named after Noah's grandson, Canaan (Genesis 10:1, 6–20). His ancestors, known as the Canaanites, lived on the land for many years. But God promised the land of Canaan to Abraham's ancestors (Genesis 15:3–7). That promise was made true when Joshua led the Israelites to take the land away from the Canaanites (Joshua 10–12).

31. CAPERNAUM

A CITY ON THE SHORE OF THE SEA OF GALILEE. Capernaum was Jesus' home during His ministry (Matthew 4:13). His disciples Andrew, Peter, and Philip moved from their hometown of Bethsaida (John 1:44) to Capernaum where disciples Matthew, James, and John lived. All of these men, except Matthew the tax collector, were fishermen (Matthew 4:18–22; 9:9). Jesus sometimes taught in the synagogue there (Mark 1:21), and did many miracles in Capernaum, including healing people and casting out demons (Matthew 8:5–17). Although the people of Capernaum saw His miracles, they did not believe in Him. Jesus scolded them for not having faith (Matthew 11:23–24).

32. CENTURION

A ROMAN SOLDIER. Centurions (Acts 10:1, 22) were military officers commanding a group of about a hundred men. There was a centurion at the foot of the cross when Jesus died. The Bible says, "With a loud cry, Jesus breathed his last. The curtain of the temple was torn in two from top to bottom. And when the centurion, who stood there in front of Jesus saw how he died, he said, 'Surely this man was the Son of God!'" (Mark 15:37–39 NIV).

33. CHERUBIM

HEAVENLY WINGED CREATURES. After God sent Adam and Eve from the Garden of Eden, the cherubim showed up. They guarded the entrance so Adam and Eve couldn't return (Genesis 3:24). Ezekiel saw cherubim, too: "Each of the winged creatures had four faces: the face of a bull, the face of a human, the face of a lion, and the face of an eagle" (Ezekiel 10:14 CEV). The ark of the covenant had golden cherubim statues on its lid (Exodus 25:18–20).

34. CIRCUMCISION

A RELIGIOUS CEREMONY PERFORMED ON BOYS. Circumcision was a symbol of God's agreement with the Israelites (Genesis 17:3–14). Israelite boys were circumcised eight days after they were born (Leviticus 12:3). The word has another meaning, too. In the New Testament, *circumcision* can mean putting off sin (Colossians 2:11).

35. COMFORTER

A NOTHER NAME FOR THE HOLY SPIRIT. The Comforter, or Holy Spirit, is our Helper. Jesus said, "I will ask the Father, and He will give you another Helper, that He may be with you forever" (John 14:16 NASB). The Holy Spirit teaches us and gives us advice, reminding us of what Jesus would do (John 14:26).

36. CONDEMNATION

THE PUNISHMENT FOR BEING GUILTY OF SIN. Everyone is guilty of sin, but Christ died so we could be forgiven (Romans 5:8). If Jesus hadn't come, we would all be condemned—no one would ever get to heaven. But Jesus came to save us from condemnation (John 3:17–18). If we truly believe in Jesus, we will live with Him forever in glory.

37. CORINTH

A COASTAL CITY NEAR ATHENS, GREECE. Corinth was known for how badly its people behaved. The apostle Paul lived in Corinth for eighteen months. He taught there, and tried to convince people to believe in Jesus. Many of the people believed and were baptized (Acts 18:1–11).

38. CORNELIUS

ONE OF THE FIRST GENTILES TO BECOME A CHRISTIAN. Cornelius was a Roman soldier, and Jews weren't supposed to interact with Gentiles like him. But Cornelius loved God, who told him to call for the apostle Peter. The Holy Spirit told Peter to accept Cornelius as a Christian. After that, other Gentiles became Christians and were baptized. Read more in Acts 10.

39. COVENANT

AN AGREEMENT OR PROMISE. God often made covenants with His people, promising to bless them if they obeyed and followed Him (Genesis 22:15–18). God made a covenant with Noah after the flood, saying, "Never again will all life be destroyed by the waters of a flood; never again will there be a flood to destroy the earth" (Genesis 9:11 NIV). God put a rainbow in the sky as a symbol of His covenant (Genesis 9:12–17). Jesus said that His blood was a covenant (Matthew 26:28), promising that those who believe in Him would be saved from condemnation (John 10:9).

40. CROSS

WHAT JESUS DIED ON. The cross was made out of two heavy wooden posts, with a long piece stuck into the ground and a shorter crosspiece toward the top. Jesus needed help to carry His cross to the place where He was crucified (Matthew 27:32). There, His hands and feet were nailed to the cross, its long post was set upright in the ground, and He was left hanging there to die (Luke 23:33). Jesus was on the cross six hours before He died (John 19:30–33). Today, we remember that event on Good Friday.

41. CUBIT

AN ANCIENT MEASUREMENT. A cubit was the length from a man's elbow to the tip of his middle finger—about 18 inches. Noah's ark was 300 cubits long, 50 cubits wide, and 30 cubits high. That comes out to about 450 feet long, 75 feet wide, and 45 feet high (Genesis 6:15).

42. DAMASCUS

THE CAPITAL CITY OF SYRIA, NORTHEAST OF JERUSALEM. Damascus is one of the world's oldest cities, and is mentioned often in the Bible—as far back as the book of Genesis (14:15). It was near Damascus that the persecutor Saul, later known as Paul, became a Christian (Acts 9:1–25).

43. DANIEL

AN OLD TESTAMENT PROPHET. Daniel was loyal to God in a time when many people worshipped false gods. God gave Daniel the gift of explaining people's dreams (Daniel 4), which sometimes predicted things that would happen in the future. Daniel is well known for being thrown into a den of lions for refusing to pray to King Darius. But God sent an angel to watch over Daniel, shutting the lions' mouths so they wouldn't eat him. Read the whole story in Daniel 6:1–24.

44. DAVID

THE MOST PROMINENT KING OF ISRAEL. David was an ancestor of Jesus (Luke 2:4–7), and like Jesus, he was born in Bethlehem (1 Samuel 17:12). As a young man, David used a sling to fight a Philistine giant named Goliath (1 Samuel 17:20–52). David was a shepherd and later a musician for King Saul (1 Samuel 16:14–21). Later, when God deposed Saul for his bad behavior, David was made the new king (1 Samuel 16:11–13). He was a very successful warrior (2 Samuel 8:1–15), and he wrote many of the psalms in the Bible.

45. DEAD SEA

A LAKE IN ISRAEL NEAR JERUSALEM. It is about fifty miles long by ten miles wide. Also known as the Sea of Salt, the lake's water is so salty that very few creatures can live in it. But the prophet Ezekiel saw a vision of a new Dead Sea, full of fresh water and many kinds of fish. The land around it will be lush and green because the water is good (Ezekiel 47:6–12).

46. DEBORAH

A JUDGE AND PROPHETESS. Deborah was a very powerful woman in Israel. She was also a military leader, as with her army's general, Barak, she battled the Canaanites and won (Judges 4:4–24). Afterward, she and Barak praised God with a song recorded in Judges 5.

47. DELILAH

S AMSON'S PHILISTINE GIRLFRIEND. Delilah was the woman who had Samson's long hair cut off. (He was sleeping when that happened.) Since, by God's design, Samson's hair gave him strength, he became very weak without it. Soon he was captured by his Philistine enemies (Judges 16:13–21).

48. DEVIL

SATAN HIMSELF. The devil wants to get people to do wrong things. He even tempted Jesus (Matthew 4:1–11), though of course, he got nowhere. Jesus is much more powerful than the devil, and wasn't fooled by his tricks. Jesus called the devil a murderer and a liar, even "the father of lies" (John 8:44). With God's help, Christians stand up to the devil's evil (Ephesians 6:10–12).

49. DISCIPLE

ONE WHO FOLLOWS JESUS. The original twelve disciples were Peter, Andrew, James the son of Zebedee, John, Philip, Bartholomew, Thomas, Matthew, James the son of Alphaeus, Thaddaeus, Simon, and Judas (Matthew 10:2–4). It was the disciples' job to spread the Gospel of Jesus Christ (John 15:16). Jesus gave His disciples the power to cast out evil spirits and to heal the sick (Matthew 10:1). Today, a disciple of Jesus is anyone who follows His teachings.

50. DOCTRINE

A SET OF IDEAS. Jesus taught about God and living the right way. Paul, Peter, and other Bible writers added to Jesus' teaching. All of their thoughts make up the Christian *doctrine*. Over the years, this doctrine has spread all over the world as people believed and became Christians.

51. Egypt

A COUNTRY IN NORTHERN AFRICA ON THE NILE RIVER. Many key Bible events took place in Egypt. Abram went there during a famine in Canaan (Genesis 12:10). Jacob's family lived in Egypt (Genesis 46:6). His ancestors became the Hebrew nation. The Hebrew people were held as slaves in Egypt for four hundred years. God told Moses to go and set them free (Exodus 3:7–10). In New Testament times, after Jesus was born, King Herod wanted Him killed—so an angel told Mary and Joseph to take Jesus to Egypt and hide (Matthew 2:13–14). Today, Egypt is a major country in Africa with a population of almost eighty million.

52. Elect

SPECIAL ONES CHOSEN BY GOD. Even before we were born, God decided whether we would believe in Him and be saved (Romans 8:29). The Bible says that God wants everyone to be saved (2 Peter 3:9), but those who refuse to believe in Jesus will be lost (John 5:39–40)—they will not go to heaven. God's chosen people should try to behave like Jesus (Romans 8:29). They should love God, love others, and live according to His rules.

53. ELIJAH

AN OLD TESTAMENT PROPHET. God told Elijah to give a message to the wicked king Ahab. The message was that no rain would fall on the king's land for three years (1 Kings 17:1). Ahab was angry, and he took it out on Elijah—so God told Elijah to hide near the Jordan River (1 Kings 17:5). There, God sent ravens to feed the prophet, who received bread and meat every day (1 Kings 17:6). Later, Elijah had a contest with King Ahab, pitting the one true God against Ahab's false god Baal, which, of course, God won (1 Kings 18:16–39). At the end of his life on earth, Elijah was taken to heaven in a very special way, as God sent a chariot and horses of fire which carried Elijah off in a whirlwind (2 Kings 2:11).

54. ELISABETH

ZACHARIAS'S WIFE AND JOHN THE BAPTIST'S MOTHER. Elisabeth was a relative of Jesus' mother, Mary. Both women were expecting babies at the same time. They knew their babies were special, because angels from the Lord had told them so (Matthew 1:20–21; Luke 1:11–13). Both women believed that the baby inside Mary was the Messiah and Savior, and they celebrated together that Jesus would soon be born (Luke 1:39–55). Elisabeth had her baby, John, first; then Jesus was born about six months later.

55. ELISHA

AN OLD TESTAMENT PROPHET. Since Elisha was the prophet Elijah's assistant, he was there to see Elijah disappear in a whirlwind. Elisha took Elijah's place as leader of the prophets (2 Kings 2:15), serving under four kings and performing numerous miracles.

56. ENOCH

A GREAT-GRANDFATHER OF NOAH (GENESIS 5:22–29). Enoch was the first son of Cain, and also the name of a city, as Cain built the city and named it after his son (Genesis 4:17). Enoch lived 365 years (Genesis 5:23), but he didn't die like a normal person. God just took him away (Genesis 5:24). This event, which theologians call "translation," is noted in the New Testament in Hebrews 11:5. It says Enoch was taken away because he was so faithful to God. Enoch had a son named Methuselah, who had the longest life span recorded in the Bible—969 years (Genesis 5:27).

57. EPISTLE

A LETTER. Many of the New Testament books are epistles. Paul wrote fourteen epistles. John wrote three. Peter wrote two. James and Jude each wrote one.

58. ESTHER

QUEEN OF PERSIA. The Old Testament book of Esther tells the story of young Esther—also called Hadassah—a Jewish orphan raised by her cousin Mordecai (Esther 2:7). After a nationwide beauty contest, she became the queen of Persia (Esther 2:17). Esther saved her people, the Jews, from an evil man named Haman, an aide to the Persian king. Because he was angry with Mordecai, Haman planned to kill all the Jews (Esther 3:5–6). When Esther found out about it, she risked her life to request the king's help. In the end, Haman was hanged and the Jews successfully defended themselves from attack.

59. EUTYCHUS

A YOUNG MAN WHO DIED DURING A SERMON. Sitting in a third-story window while the apostle Paul was preaching, Eutychus fell asleep, dropped to the ground, and died. He was picked up, dead, but Paul put his arms around Eutychus and said, "Don't worry! He's alive" (Acts 20:9–10 CEV). The people were "not a little comforted" (Acts 20:12 KJV).

60. EVE

THE FIRST WOMAN. Eve is sometimes called the mother of the human race (Genesis 3:20). God made her from one of Adam's ribs (Genesis 2:21–22) so that Adam would have a helper. They lived in a garden called Eden, with freedom to eat from any tree except one—the tree of the knowledge of good and evil (Genesis 2:17). One day, a serpent—Satan in disguise—approached Eve to tempt her to eat the forbidden fruit. She did, and she also gave some to Adam (Genesis 3:1–6). God was angry that Eve and Adam had disobeyed, and pronounced a curse on the ground. God told Adam and Eve that they would have to work hard for the rest of their lives (Genesis 3:19). Then He sent them out of the garden forever (Genesis 3:23).

61. EZEKIEL

A PROPHET, PRIEST, AND AUTHOR. God allowed Ezekiel to "see" things that would happen in the future (Ezekiel 1:3). He wrote the Old Testament book called by his name. It predicted things that were to come. Most of Ezekiel's predictions were about Israel and the Jewish people, though some of his predictions have yet to come true. They refer to the end times when Jesus will come back to earth.

62. FAITH

CONFIDENCE IN SOMETHING YOU'VE BEEN TOLD. *Faith* is another word for trust. It's believing in God, even though you can't see Him (Hebrews 11:1). Like the air we breathe, God can't be seen—but we know by faith they're there. Jesus said anything is possible when we put our faith in God (Mark 9:23). The very first point of faith is this: to believe that Jesus was sent by God to save us from our sins. If we have faith in Him, our souls won't die. Instead, we'll live forever with God (John 3:16).

63. FALL OF MAN

WHEN ADAM AND EVE MADE A HUGE MISTAKE BY DISOBEYING GOD. Adam and Eve were the first people on earth, and God gave them just one rule to obey: They could not eat fruit from a particular tree in the Garden of Eden. As created, Adam and Eve knew only good things—but by eating that fruit, they would know the difference between good and evil. The "fall of man" came when Satan got Eve to taste the fruit. She then gave some to Adam, who ate it, too. As punishment, God sent Adam and Eve out of the garden forever (Genesis 3). Since that time, all humans know good from evil and have a choice to obey or disobey God. Sadly, there is not one person on earth who has not disobeyed (Romans 3:23).

64. FAMINE

A WIDESPREAD LACK OF FOOD. There were many famines in Bible times. Some were caused when there wasn't enough rain. Others were caused by hailstorms (Exodus 9:23), insects (Exodus 10:13–15), and enemies (Deuteronomy 28:49–51). When the Israelites were in the Desert of Sin, they were starving until God made manna appear on the ground (Exodus 16:4).

65. FAST

To STOP EATING OR DRINKING FOR A WHILE. Fasting was common in Bible times, and some people still fast today as a way to be close to God. Leaders in Bible times sometimes ordered people to fast (Ezra 8:21). Jesus Himself fasted (Luke 4:1–4), teaching that when people fast, they should do it in secret (Matthew 6:16–18). In other words, fasting should be a private thing between a person and God, not something done for show.

66. FIRMAMENT

The sky. *Firmament* is an Old Testament word for the heavens, or the sky above the earth (Genesis 1:6–8 KJV).

67. FLOOD, THE

GOD'S DO-OVER IN THE TIME OF NOAH (GENESIS 6–9). After Adam and Eve sinned in the Garden of Eden, human beings went downhill fast. God decided to wipe out the whole earth with a massive flood. Only Noah, seven members of his family, and pairs of certain animals survived in a giant boat Noah built (the ark). When the flood went away—about a year later—the people and animals were to start over and refill the earth with life. God told Noah He would never flood the earth again, and sealed that promise with a rainbow (Genesis 9:13–17).

68. FOOT-WASHING

WASHING THE FEET OF GUESTS IN YOUR HOME. In Bible times, since people's feet got really dirty on the dry, dusty walking paths, hosts washed their visitors' feet. It was a way of saying, "Welcome to our home." Though servants usually did the foot-washing, Jesus washed His disciples' feet to teach them a lesson: they weren't to think that they were better than anyone else (John 13:1–17).

69. FORGIVENESS

OVERLOOKING THE WRONG ANOTHER PERSON HAS DONE. Forgiveness can be hard, especially if the offense was a bad one. But Jesus said if we forgive others for the bad things *they* do, God will forgive *us* for the bad things we do (Matthew 6:14–15). Jesus came to earth to take the punishment for our sins (Acts 10:43)—God's forgiveness for those who ask Him. As forgiven people, we can ask God to help us forgive others (Matthew 6:12).

70. Gabriel

An important angel (Luke 1:19). Gabriel brought messages from God, and appeared a few times in the Bible. The prophet Daniel saw him twice. Gabriel helped him understand his dreams (Daniel 8:15–17; Daniel 9:21–24). Gabriel appeared to Zechariah, too, telling him that his son would grow up to be John the Baptist (Luke 1:11–19). And Gabriel appeared to Mary, Jesus' mother, saying that she would give birth to Jesus, the Son of God (Luke 1:26–45).

71. Garden of Eden

Adam and Eve's first home. A river flowed through the garden, splitting into four other rivers: the Pishon and Gihon (which no longer exist) and the Tigris and Euphrates. The garden had many trees, but there was one particular tree Adam and Eve could not eat from—the "tree of the knowledge of good and evil" (Genesis 2:9). When they broke God's rule and ate fruit from the forbidden tree, they brought sin and death into the world (Romans 5:12). God made them leave the garden forever (Genesis 3).

72. Gentiles

People who are not of the Jewish race. In Bible times, Jews looked down on Gentiles, viewing them as "unclean." In fact, it was against the law for a Jew to even visit a Gentile (Acts 10:28). But Jesus changed that. His death and resurrection allowed *everyone* to be forgiven for their sins, if they ask (Galatians 3:28). When the Gentiles first heard that Jesus died for their sins, too, they were very glad (Acts 13:46–48).

73. GETHSEMANE

A GARDEN OUTSIDE JERUSALEM. The Garden of Gethsemane is a famous place near the Mount of Olives. Jesus prayed there the night He was arrested. Earlier, as Jesus ate supper with His disciples, He told them He was about to be arrested and killed. When He went into the Garden of Gethsemane to pray, He was very sad (Mark 14:33–34), saying to God, "My Father, if it is possible, don't make me suffer by having me drink from this cup. But do what you want, and not what I want" (Matthew 26:39 CEV). A short time later, Jesus was arrested and taken away (John 18:1–12).

74. GIDEON

A FAITHFUL HERO OF THE OLD TESTAMENT (HEBREWS 11:32–34). Gideon was a leader in Israel, called by God to fight the powerful Midianite army (Judges 6:14–16) which God had been using to punish Israel for its sins (Judges 6:1). When Gideon and his servants destroyed an altar to the false god Baal, replacing it with one to honor God (Judges 6:25–27), the Midianites were moved to attack. They came after Gideon with a huge army, "thick as locusts" (Judges 7:12 NIV). Gideon had more than thirty thousand men in his army, but God narrowed that group down to just three hundred, to show the Israelites that they shouldn't trust in their own power. With that tiny army—and God's intervention—Gideon defeated the Midianites (Judges 7:16–25).

75. GLEANING

GATHERING LEFTOVER CROPS. The Bible describes harvesters who went into fields to pick grain, and the poor people who were allowed to follow them to collect the leftovers (Leviticus 19:9–10). In the Bible story of Ruth, she was gleaning barley and wheat from a field that belonged to a man named Boaz (Ruth 2).

76. GOD

THE CREATOR AND RULER OF THE UNIVERSE (ISAIAH 40:28). God is the ultimate reality (Isaiah 40:18). He can do anything and everything (Jeremiah 32:17). God is our heavenly Father (Matthew 6:9), who knows all our weaknesses (Psalm 103:14), thoughts (Psalm 44:21), and words (Psalm 139:4). He knows our actions (Psalm 139:2) and our needs (Matthew 6:32). God is so great that He is everywhere at the same time (Jeremiah 23:23–24). He is more powerful than anything else (Revelation 19:6), yet forgiving, wise, and truthful (Psalm 136; Colossians 2:2–3; Titus 1:2). God loved people so much that He sent His Son Jesus to earth to save us from our sins. He promised that if we believe in Jesus, our souls will live forever with Him (John 3:16).

77. Golden Calf

An idol Aaron made. In Bible times, people created false gods and worshipped them, making the true God angry. Aaron, Moses' brother, foolishly made a golden calf for the Israelites. He was waiting with the people while Moses was on the mountain with God, receiving the Ten Commandments. When Moses was away for a long time, the people lost faith and asked Aaron to make a god to lead them. Aaron fashioned a golden calf out of the Israelites' jewelry. The people bowed down and worshipped the statue, infuriating God. Read the whole story in Exodus 32.

78. Goliath

A giant more than nine feet tall. Goliath was a Philistine warrior from the city of Gath. He fought with the Philistine army in a great war with the Israelites. Every day, Goliath dared the Israelites to choose a soldier to fight him one-on-one, but no Jewish soldier wanted to. "He wore a bronze helmet and had bronze armor to protect his chest and legs. The chest armor alone weighed about one hundred twenty-five pounds. He carried a bronze sword strapped on his back, and his spear was so big that the iron spearhead alone weighed more than fifteen pounds" (1 Samuel 17:5–7 CEV). But David, a brave young shepherd boy, volunteered to fight Goliath—and with just a slingshot and a stone, he killed the giant. Read more in 1 Samuel 17.

79. GOSPEL

THE "GOOD NEWS" (MARK 1:15); NAMELY, THAT JESUS DIED SO WE CAN LIVE FOREVER! God sent His Son, Jesus, into the world to live among the people. While He was here, Jesus taught about God. Then He died on a cross as a sacrifice for sin, and three days later rose from the dead to prove His power over death (Luke 24:3–8). Jesus promised that whoever believes in Him will not die, but will live forever with God (John 3:16).

80. GRACE

GOD'S FAVOR THAT WE DON'T DESERVE. Our sins offend God. But grace is given to those who believe in Jesus (Titus 2:11). There is no way humans can be perfect like God. Everyone sins (1 John 1:8). After Adam and Eve disobeyed God, humans were punished for their sins. In the Old Testament, people had to sacrifice animals to become right with God. But Jesus changed that by dying on the cross (Romans 4:25). He took the blame for the bad things we do—and if we believe in Jesus, by the grace of God we are saved (Ephesians 2:4–6). Grace is a gift from God (Ephesians 2:8).

81. HANNAH

THE PROPHET SAMUEL'S MOTHER. Hannah was barren, but when she asked God for a son, He said yes. Hannah promised God that her son would be faithful and serve Him, so she allowed the priest Eli to raise Samuel in the tabernacle, where the people of Israel went to worship God. Hannah's beautiful prayer, thanking God for His blessings, is recorded in 1 Samuel 2:1–10.

82. HEAVEN

GOD'S HOME (1 KINGS 8:34). Jesus said He was going to heaven to prepare a place for us. He promised to come back for us so we can be with Him always (John 14:2–3). Heaven is a place of great reward (Matthew 5:12).

83. HELL

WHERE UNBELIEVERS GO WHEN THEY DIE. Hell is the antithesis of heaven. A terrible place, hell is described as a land of "fire that shall never be quenched" (Mark 9:43 NKJV) and where people are shut away from God and His kindness (2 Thessalonians 1:9).

84. HERESY

BELIEFS AND TEACHINGS ABOUT GOD AND THE BIBLE THAT AREN'T TRUE. The Bible often uses the phrase "false teachers" to describe people who promote heresy: "But there were false prophets also among the people, even as there shall be false teachers among you, who privily shall bring in damnable heresies, even denying the Lord that bought them, and bring upon themselves swift destruction. And many shall follow their pernicious ways" (2 Peter 2:1–2 KJV).

85. HEZEKIAH

THE TUNNELING KING. Hezekiah was a godly king in Jerusalem, one who stopped his people from worshipping idols. He also took advice from God's prophet Isaiah (Isaiah 38:1–8). When Hezekiah thought the Assyrian army might attack Jerusalem, he worried that he and his people would be trapped inside. So he ordered a tunnel dug through solid rock from the city to a spring outside to carry water into Jerusalem. If they were trapped inside, there would be water to drink (2 Chronicles 32:30). It also left less water for the Assyrians to use (2 Chronicles 32:2–4).

86. HIGH PRIEST

THE LEADER OF THE PRIESTS. Aaron, Moses' older brother, was the first high priest of Israel. When he died, his son, Eleazar, became high priest. This continued through the generations, as all the high priests of Israel were descendants of Aaron (Exodus 28). Jesus Christ is called the "great high priest" (Hebrews 4:14), because He gave His own life as a sacrifice for all people (Hebrews 9:26).

87. HOLY SPIRIT

GOD'S THIRD "PERSON." God is three persons in one: God the Father, Jesus the Son, and the Holy Spirit (Matthew 28:19). The Holy Spirit's purpose is to help and support all the people who believe in God (John 14:12–27). After Jesus died and ascended to heaven, He sent the Holy Spirit to be with His followers (Acts 2:1–21). The Holy Spirit is sometimes called the *Helper*, and one of His jobs is to help people understand what's in the Bible (1 Corinthians 2:13). He's also called the *Comforter* (John 14:16) because He encourages us in hard times. The Holy Spirit can convict nonbelievers of their sin (John 16:8), so they might believe in Jesus and be saved.

88. HOSANNA

A SHOUT OF PRAISE TO GOD. *Hosanna* means "save us now." It's what the crowd shouted when Jesus rode into Jerusalem on a young donkey (Matthew 21:9). Today, we celebrate that day as Palm Sunday.

89. HOSEA

AN OLD TESTAMENT BOOK NAMED FOR THE PROPHET WHO WROTE IT. Hosea preached to the northern kingdom of Israel. God told Hosea that He would allow His people to be punished by their enemies for a while. Then God would save them from the punishment (Hosea 4–14). Hosea is probably best known for marrying a "wife of whoredoms" (Hosea 1:2) at God's command. Their marriage—a faithful husband and an adulterous wife—pictured God's relationship to Israel.

90. I Am

GOD'S SPECIAL NAME FOR HIMSELF. When God spoke to Moses through a burning bush, He called Himself *I AM*. God said, "This is my name forever, the name you shall call me from generation to generation" (Exodus 3:15 NIV). Since God has always existed and will continue forever (Revelation 1:8), He simply *is*. Many people call Jesus "the Great I Am," since He used the words "I am" several times to describe Himself in the Gospel of John (John 6:35, 8:12, 10:7, 10:11, 11:25, 14:6, and 15:5).

91. Idol

ANYTHING WORSHIPPED THAT IS NOT GOD (ROMANS 1:25). In Bible times, there were many instances of idol worship. Many people—even Israelites—worshipped a false god named Baal (Numbers 25:3). Exodus 32 describes Aaron's mistake in making a golden calf for Israel. Other idols were made from different kinds of metal and wood. The first of God's Ten Commandments says: "You shall have no other gods before Me" (Exodus 20:3). Idol worship makes God jealous and angry (Psalm 78:58).

92. INSPIRATION

GOD LEADING PEOPLE TO DO GOOD THINGS. God inspires people in many ways. He "breathed out" (the literal meaning of *inspired*) the content of scripture (2 Timothy 3:16). He spoke to prophets and sent them into the world with His messages (1 Samuel 19:20). A few times, God talked out loud to people (Exodus 3). He also inspired through dreams (Daniel 1:17) and visions (Ezekiel 11:24–25). And He gives wisdom to help us understand today (Job 32:8).

93. ISAAC

ABRAHAM AND SARAH'S SON. When Isaac was born, his parents were very old—Abraham was a hundred (Genesis 21:5) and Sarah was ninety (Genesis 17:17). When Isaac was a boy, God decided to test Abraham's faith by asking Abraham to offer his son as a sacrifice (Genesis 22:1–2). Abraham was ready to do what God asked when an angel of the Lord appeared. "Don't hurt the boy!" the angel said (Genesis 22:12 CEV). Isaac's life was spared, and he grew up and married a girl named Rebekah (Genesis 25:20). They had twin boys named Jacob and Esau (Genesis 25:23–26), both of whom started great nations—Jacob, the nation of Israel.

94. ISAIAH

AN OLD TESTAMENT PROPHET. Isaiah worked in the city of
Jerusalem, giving messages from God to King Uzziah and
the kings who followed him. Isaiah warned that the Assyrians
would destroy Jerusalem and Israel, but he added that some
of God's people would be saved (Isaiah 1:2–9, 11:11). He
predicted King Hezekiah's death, then told the king that God
was going to give him fifteen more years to live (2 Kings 20).
Isaiah also predicted Jesus' birth (Isaiah 7:14). Isaiah described
a man who would tell people to prepare for Jesus (Isaiah 40:3).
That man was John the Baptist (Matthew 3:1–3).

95. ISRAEL

A VERY IMPORTANT BIBLE NAME. *Israel* had three usages in
scripture. First, it was a new name God gave Jacob, after
Jacob wrestled all night with God at a place called Penuel
(Genesis 32:24–32). Second, Jacob's twelve sons and all their
descendants became a nation called "Israel" after Jacob's new
name. Third, a smaller nation of Israel formed in 931 BC when
ten tribes split from the twelve tribes of Israel. They created
their own nation with its own king, Jeroboam (1 Kings 12),
and a capital city of Samaria. This Israel existed for about two
hundred years before it was overrun by Assyria in 722 BC (2
Kings 17:23–24).

96. JACOB

THE SON OF ISAAC AND REBEKAH. Jacob and his brother, Esau, were twins. Esau was the older of the two (Genesis 25:24–26), and as the oldest, was promised a special blessing after his father's death. But he sold his right to the fortune to his younger brother, Jacob, for a bowl of stew (Genesis 25:29–34)! Jacob had schemed to steal his father's blessing, and Esau was so angry he decided to kill Jacob (see Genesis 27:1–41). When their mother found out, she sent Jacob to live with an uncle (Genesis 27:42–46). On his way there, Jacob had a dream of a ladder to heaven with angels going up and down. God spoke to Jacob, promising him land and many ancestors. Read more in Genesis 28:10–15. Jacob grew up, got married, and had a large family. God changed Jacob's name to Israel (Genesis 32:28), and all of his ancestors were known as the Israelites. His son Joseph became important in the kingdom of Egypt.

97. JAMES

A DISCIPLE OF JESUS. James lived in Capernaum and worked as a fisherman. He was at the Sea of Galilee when Jesus chose him as a disciple, along with James's younger brother, John (Matthew 4:21). Jesus called the brothers "Sons of Thunder" (Mark 3:17), perhaps because they had strong tempers. James shared many important moments with Jesus: He was there when God appeared to Jesus in a bright cloud, saying, "This is my Son, whom I love; with him I am well pleased" (Matthew 17:5 NIV). James was also present when Jesus brought a dead girl back to life (Luke 8:49–56) and when the Lord was transfigured (Mark 9:2). James was also with Jesus the night He was arrested (Mark 14:33).

98. JEREMIAH

A PROPHET IN OLD TESTAMENT TIMES. God chose Jeremiah even before he was born (Jeremiah 1:4–5). When he grew up, he was sad that the Israelites were behaving so badly (Jeremiah 9:1), and became known as the "weeping prophet." Jeremiah warned the people, saying God would punish them for their behavior (Jeremiah 16:1–21). But the people didn't listen, and even turned against Jeremiah, plotting to kill him (Jeremiah 11:21). Even Jeremiah's family turned on him (Jeremiah 12:6). But God did what He promised through Jeremiah: the Babylonians took over the land, and the people were taken away as prisoners (Jeremiah 27:6).

99. JERICHO

AN ANCIENT WALLED CITY. Jericho was near the Jordan River and the Dead Sea. Joshua captured Jericho when the Israelites entered the Promised Land (Joshua 6:1–22)—his faith in God made the walls around the city fall down (Hebrews 11:30)! In New Testament times, Jesus visited Jericho, where He taught and healed people. This was where Jesus gave sight to the blind man, Bartimaeus (Mark 10:46–52). Jericho was also the place where Zacchaeus climbed a tree to better see Jesus (Luke 19:1–9).

100. JERUSALEM

A FAMOUS CITY, BOTH IN BIBLE TIMES AND TODAY. Jerusalem
is an ancient city, the most important city to the Jewish
people. Jerusalem existed when the first book of the Bible,
Genesis, was written. At that time, it was called Salem (Genesis
14:18). Later known as Jebus (Judges 19:10), Jerusalem gained
its current name by the time of the sixth book of the Bible,
Joshua (Joshua 10:1). Jerusalem was the site of God's temple
(1 Kings 3:1; 6:1–38), and was fought over often. Jesus cried
because Jerusalem was sinful (Luke 19:41–42), and rode
into the city on a young donkey (Matthew 21:1–11). He
was crucified just outside Jerusalem's city walls (Luke 23:33).
Someday, God will create a perfect city where there will be no
sin, calling it "the new Jerusalem" (Revelation 21:2).

101. JESUS CHRIST

SON OF GOD; SAVIOR OF THE WORLD. Jesus was born in Bethlehem to a young woman named Mary (Luke 2:4–7, 21). His father is God through a miraculous conception in Mary, who was a virgin. Her husband, Joseph, acted as Jesus' father on earth.

When Jesus was born, King Herod was jealous, fearing Jesus would challenge his position. So Herod plotted to kill Jesus. When an angel warned Mary and Joseph, they ran away with Jesus to Egypt, and His life was spared (Matthew 2:13–14).

As a man, Jesus taught crowds of people about God. He chose twelve men—His disciples—to help Him (Matthew 10:1–4). Jesus taught truths about God and His kingdom, healed the sick, and performed many other miracles. The people were amazed at what He could do. Many believed Jesus was the Son of God, though others rejected Him.

The Jewish leaders were jealous of Jesus and wanted Him killed (Matthew 26:3–4). When they saw an opportunity, they arrested Jesus and accused Him of blasphemy for claiming to be God's Son (Mark 14:55–65). Jesus was crucified; then His body was put in a tomb (John 19). Three days later, though, Jesus came back to life and appeared to many people over a period of forty days (Acts 1:3). After one last meeting with His disciples, Jesus ascended to heaven on a cloud (Luke 24:36–51).

Jesus' death was part of God the Father's plan. God sacrificed Jesus, His own Son, to save people from sin (Mark 10:45). When Jesus died, He took all of our sins on Himself; when He came back to life, He proved that He is the Son of God. If we believe in what Jesus did, God will forgive us for our sins (Acts 16:31). Jesus promised to come back to earth someday, to take all who believe in Him to heaven.

102. JEZEBEL

KING AHAB'S WICKED WIFE. Queen Jezebel persuaded the Israelites to worship the false god Baal, and killed some of God's prophets (1 Kings 18:4). Then, another of God's prophets, Elijah, predicted that Jezebel would be killed. Furious, Jezebel planned to kill Elijah (1 Kings 19:1–2), but he escaped. When a new king, Jehu, came to power, he had Jezebel and her whole family executed (2 Kings 9:30–37). No one from her family ever ruled Israel again.

103. JOB

A MAN FAMOUS FOR SUFFERING. Job was a very good man (Job 1:1) with a large family and extensive property—in sheep, camels, cows, and servants. When Satan said Job served God only for His blessings, God let Satan attack Job's possessions. First, Job lost his children, animals, and servants. Then, with God's permission, Satan attacked Job's health. But Job refused to "curse God and die," as his wife suggested (Job 2:9). The old phrase "the patience of Job" isn't entirely true, because Job spent a lot of time complaining to God. In the end, though, Job learned that God knows best, even when we suffer. God returned to Job the possessions he'd lost (and more), even giving him ten more children (Job 42).

104. JOHN

JESUS' CLOSEST FRIEND. John was one of Jesus' twelve disciples. He lived in Capernaum and fished on the shores of the Sea of Galilee. John's father was Zebedee, and his brother, James, another disciple (Matthew 4:21–22). He might have had a temper, since Jesus called John and his brother James "Sons of Thunder" (Mark 3:17). John described himself as "the disciple whom Jesus loved" (John 19:26). After Jesus returned to heaven, John wrote one of the four Gospels. He also wrote three New Testament letters and the book of Revelation.

105. John the Baptist

A PROPHET WHO PREPARED THE WAY FOR JESUS. The son of Zacharias and Elisabeth, John was also related to Jesus. The Old Testament prophet Isaiah made predictions about John: "Someone is shouting: 'Clear a path in the desert! Make a straight road for the LORD our God' " (Isaiah 40:3 CEV). Some seven hundred years later, those predictions came true as John the Baptist began preaching in the desert (Matthew 3:1–3), preparing the way for Jesus.

John wore clothes made of camel's hair and ate grasshoppers and wild honey. Crowds of people came to him to be baptized in the Jordan River. In fact, John even baptized Jesus, though reluctantly. He didn't think he was worthy to baptize such a great man (Matthew 3:13–15).

John criticized King Herod for marrying his brother's wife, so the king threw John into prison (Luke 3:19–20). Later, at his wife's instigation, Herod had John killed. Jesus said of John, "Truly I tell you, among those born of women there has not risen anyone greater than John the Baptist" (Matthew 11:11 NIV).

106. JONAH

A PROPHET SWALLOWED BY A BIG FISH. God told Jonah to go to Nineveh and preach repentance to its wicked people (Jonah 1:1–2). But Jonah didn't want to go. Instead, he ran away.

Jonah boarded a boat headed toward Spain (Jonah 1:3). On the way, a huge storm came up, and even the pagan sailors sensed that God was punishing someone on board. Jonah admitted that he was running from God, and the sailors—at his request—reluctantly threw him overboard (Jonah 1:8–15). God had prepared a giant fish to swallow Jonah (Jonah 1:17), and he sat in the fish's belly for three days and nights. All the while, he prayed to God. Finally, the fish spit Jonah out onto the shore (Jonah 2:10).

After that, Jonah obeyed God, going to Nineveh to preach. The Ninevites changed their ways, and God was pleased (Jonah 3). Strangely, though, the book ends with Jonah pouting, as he had hoped for the destruction of the wicked city. But God showed His heart for all people in the final words of the book: "And should I not have concern for the great city of Nineveh, in which there are more than a hundred and twenty thousand people who cannot tell their right hand from their left—and also many animals?" (Jonah 4:11 NIV).

107. Jordan River

THE LARGEST AND MOST IMPORTANT RIVER IN ISRAEL. The Jordan River starts in Syria and flows about two hundred miles south through the Sea of Galilee to the northern end of the Dead Sea. The river and the land around it are mentioned often in the Bible—about two hundred times. This is where the Israelites crossed into the Promised Land (Joshua 3:15–17). It is also where John the Baptist preached and baptized people. The river is best known as the place where John baptized Jesus (Matthew 3:13–17).

108. Joseph

A NAME SHARED BY SEVERAL MEN IN THE BIBLE. Four were notable: One was married to Jesus' mother, Mary. He served as Jesus' adoptive dad, since Jesus' birth father was God Himself (Matthew 1:20–25). Another Joseph, the son of the Old Testament patriarch Jacob, was sold as a slave (Genesis 37:12–36), but later became an important leader in the Egyptian pharaoh's kingdom. The third Joseph was a man from Arimathea. Jesus was buried in this Joseph's tomb (Matthew 27:57–61). Another Joseph almost became the twelfth disciple to replace the wicked Judas Iscariot. But the job went to another man, named Matthias (Acts 1:23–26).

109. JOSHUA

MOSES' SUCCESSOR AS LEADER OF THE ISRAELITES. Joshua led God's people into the Promised Land (Joshua 1:1–6) after overrunning the walled city of Jericho. God gave Joshua an unusual plan for capturing the city: Joshua and his army marched around the perimeter for six days. Then, on the seventh day, they blew trumpets and shouted, and the walls came crashing down (Joshua 6:1–20). Joshua was a strong leader who seemed to do everything right—the Bible never records a sinful episode with him. He died at age 110 (Joshua 24:29).

110. JUDAH

THE SOUTHERN JEWISH KINGDOM. When King Solomon died, the Israelites split into two kingdoms. The northern kingdom kept the name Israel. The southern kingdom, called Judah, had its capital at Jerusalem (1 Kings 14:21). At many times in their history, the people of Judah worshipped idols and otherwise disrespected God. So He allowed the Babylonian army to destroy Jerusalem. Babylon took the people away and made them slaves; though, years later, some of the people came back to rebuild the city (2 Chronicles 36:20–23).

111. Judas Iscariot

THE DISCIPLE WHO BETRAYED JESUS. He seemed trustworthy—in fact, he was keeper of the disciples' money (John 13:29). But Judas was the one who betrayed Jesus to the high priests and elders for thirty silver coins (Matthew 26:14–15). After Jesus was arrested, Judas felt remorse and tried to give the money back. But the religious leaders refused, and Judas decided to kill himself. The place where he died is called the Field of Blood (Matthew 27:1–10).

112. Judgment, Last

THE DAY WHEN GOD SEPARATES THE SAVED FROM THE LOST. At the end of time, Jesus will return to gather all His people and take them away to heaven. Everyone who does not believe will be judged (Matthew 25:31–33). Though it will be a wonderful day for those who believe, it will be terrible for nonbelievers (Romans 2:5–8). No one knows exactly when Jesus will return, so the Bible says to be prepared (1 Thessalonians 5:1–11).

113. JUSTIFICATION

BEING MADE RIGHT WITH GOD. Humans can't be right with God by their own accomplishments or good works. We are only justified by believing in Jesus Christ (Romans 4:25). When we are right with God, we are at peace with Him—and we have the hope of living with Him in heaven (Titus 3:5–7).

114. KINGDOM OF GOD

THE RULE OF GOD IN CHRISTIANS' HEARTS (LUKE 17:20–21). Jesus preached what Mark called "the gospel of the kingdom of God" (Mark 1:14). Jesus taught His disciples to seek God's kingdom (Matthew 6:33) and pray for it to come to earth (Matthew 6:10).

115. Lamb of God

A NAME USED FOR CHRIST. In Bible times, lambs were often used for sacrifices. This name fits Jesus well because His death was a sacrifice for sins. The prophet Isaiah compared Jesus' death to the death of a lamb: "He was silent like a lamb being led to the butcher, as quiet as a sheep having its wool cut off" (Isaiah 53:7 CEV). When John the Baptist saw Jesus, he said, "Here is the Lamb of God who takes away the sin of the world!" (John 1:29 CEV). In heaven, Jesus is praised as the Lamb of God (Revelation 5:12–13).

116. Lazarus

MARY AND MARTHA'S BROTHER. When Jesus heard that Lazarus was sick, He said, "His sickness won't end in death. It will bring glory to God and his Son" (John 11:4 CEV). After Lazarus died, Jesus brought him back to life, and many who saw the miracle put their faith in Christ. Others were angry, though, the Jewish leaders making plans to kill Jesus (John 11:41–53). They planned to kill Lazarus, too, blaming him for making so many people put their faith in Jesus (John 12:10–11).

117. LEPROSY

SKIN DISEASES. Those with leprosy were called *lepers*, and in Bible times, people feared them. Lepers had to follow special rules, including living apart from others. They also had to shout, "Unclean!" wherever they went so non-lepers could stay away from them (Leviticus 13:45–46). But Jesus was kind to lepers, as He was to many of the sick and possessed. Once, ten lepers asked for Jesus' help and He healed them all (Luke 17:11–14). Jesus gave His disciples the power to heal (Matthew 10:1), and specifically mentioned cleansing lepers (Matthew 10:8).

118. LORD'S DAY

SUNDAY, THE FIRST DAY OF THE WEEK. The Lord's day (Revelation 1:10) is also the day that most Christians worship God in churches. People of the Jewish faith worship on Saturday, the last day of the week, called the Sabbath. After Jesus rose from the dead on the first day of the week, Christians made Sunday their normal day for worship (Acts 20:7). In AD 321, the Roman emperor Constantine made it a Christian holiday.

119. LOT

ABRAHAM'S NEPHEW. Lot went with his uncle Abraham to Canaan (Genesis 12:5). Abraham let Lot choose where to live in Canaan, and Lot picked the lush Jordan Valley (Genesis 13:10–11). Unfortunately, that was near the wicked city of Sodom. In time, God decided to destroy Sodom for its sins, but He sent an angel to save Lot's family. The angel told them to run and not look back. Lot and his two daughters escaped, but his wife didn't—she looked back and was turned into a pillar of salt. Read more in Genesis 19:15–26.

120. LUKE

A CHRISTIAN DOCTOR (COLOSSIANS 4:14) AND AUTHOR OF TWO NEW TESTAMENT BOOKS. Luke wrote the third and longest Gospel and the book of Acts. Born a Gentile (which means his family was not Jewish), he also went with Paul on some of his missionary trips (Acts 16:10). Luke was the last to stay with Paul before he died (2 Timothy 4:11).

121. LYDIA

A BUSINESSWOMAN OF THE BIBLE. Lydia lived in the city of Thyatira where she sold purple cloth. After Lydia heard Paul preach in Philippi, she and her household were baptized and became Christians. She asked Paul and his friends to stay at her home (Acts 16:14–15).

122. MANNA

M IRACLE FOOD. God gave the Israelites manna when they were in the wilderness. In Hebrew, the word *manna* means, "What is it?" In the Bible, it's called "bread from heaven" (Exodus 16:4), and described as tiny white seeds that "tasted like something baked with sweet olive oil" (Numbers 11:8 CEV). The people would grind or crush the seeds into flour. Then they would "boil it and make it into thin wafers" (Numbers 11:9 CEV).

123. MARK

A COUSIN OF BARNABAS (COLOSSIANS 4:10). Mark went with Barnabas and Paul on the first mission trip (Acts 12:25). Mark went as far as Perga, then turned back to Jerusalem (Acts 13:3–13). Because of Mark's vacillation, Paul wouldn't let him go on the next trip. Barnabas, who wanted to take Mark, parted ways with Paul (Acts 15:36–41). Mark's mother was a Christian woman named Mary, and people who followed the Lord went to her home to pray (Acts 12:12). Mark is believed to be the author of the second Gospel.

124. MARY

A NAME SHARED BY MANY WOMEN IN THE BIBLE. The most well known are Jesus' mother and Mary Magdalene. Jesus' mother, often called "the Virgin Mary," was engaged to Joseph. An angel told her she would give birth to Jesus (Luke 1:26–35). She followed her Son's ministry through the years, and witnessed His crucifixion, when Jesus put her into the care of His disciple John (John 19:26–27). Mary Magdalene, the other Mary, also saw Jesus being crucified (Matthew 27:55–61). When she saw His empty tomb, she told the disciples (John 20:1–2). This Mary was one of the first to see Jesus after He'd risen from the dead (Mark 16:9). A third Mary was the sister of Martha and Lazarus. She listened to Jesus' teaching while her sister busied herself with hostessing (Luke 10:38–39). Mary once poured perfume on Jesus' feet and wiped them with her hair (John 12:1–3).

125. MATTHEW

A TAX COLLECTOR WHO BECAME ONE OF JESUS' TWELVE DISCIPLES (MATTHEW 9:9). He wrote the first book in the New Testament, a job made easier by his unpopular career choice. Those who collected taxes had to be good at keeping records, and that made Matthew a good choice for a writer. Some people called Matthew "Levi" (Mark 2:13–17; Luke 5:27–32). The proud Pharisees lumped Matthew (a "publican") with other "sinners" that Jesus ate with (Matthew 9:11).

126. MELCHIZEDEK

AN ANCIENT KING AND PRIEST. Abraham gave Melchizedek a tenth of all he had (Genesis 14:18–20). A mysterious figure, we don't know about Melchizedek's parents or his death (Hebrews 7:3), but the Bible says his priesthood is endless (Hebrews 7:16). In the book of Psalms, King David said the Messiah would be a priest forever, just like this king (Psalm 110:4).

127. MERCY SEAT

THE LID OF THE ARK OF THE COVENANT (EXODUS 25:17–21). It was made out of pure gold, with two carved angels facing each other. The Lord told Moses, "I will meet you there between the two creatures and tell you what my people must do and what they must not do" (Exodus 25:22 CEV). Once a year, the high priest sprinkled blood from a sacrificed bull and goat on the seat. This was done for his sins and the sins of the people (Leviticus 16:11–16).

128. METHUSELAH

A SON OF ENOCH (GENESIS 5:21) AND NOAH'S GRANDFATHER. He lived to be 969 years old (Genesis 5:27), the longest life span recorded in the Bible.

129. MIRACLE

AN ACT OF GOD THAT GOES AGAINST THE LAWS OF NATURE. In the New Testament, miracles are called signs, wonders, mighty works, and powers. Most miracles took place in one of five biblical periods. The first period was the Exodus (Exodus 7, 9, 10, 14). The next was during the lives of Elijah (1 Kings 18:30–39) and Elisha (2 Kings 4:2–7). The third period was during the Exile (Daniel 3:9–27). The fourth was Jesus' time—His miracles were signs that He possessed God's power (Matthew 15:33–39) to heal the sick (Matthew 8:14–17), give life to the dead (Matthew 9:23–25), even calm the wind and sea (Luke 8:22–25). The fifth period was the time of the apostles' work. Their miracles proved they were disciples of Jesus (Acts 3:6–9).

130. MOSES

A PROPHET OF ISRAEL WHO WROTE THE FIRST FIVE BOOKS OF THE BIBLE. Moses was a Hebrew, born in Egypt during the Israelites' years of slavery there. He spent the first forty years of his life in Egypt, after escaping the Pharaoh's order that all the Hebrew boy babies should be killed (Exodus 1:16). Moses' mother put him in a basket along the Nile River, where the king's daughter found and adopted him. Read more in Exodus 2:1–10. Years later, after killing an Egyptian who was mistreating a Hebrew slave, Moses ran away into the desert (Exodus 2:12–15).

Moses spent the next forty years in Midian, married a woman named Zipporah, and had two sons (Exodus 18:2–4). God called Moses to go back to Egypt to lead the Israelites out of slavery (Exodus 3:11–4:20). God sent ten plagues on Egypt to convince the Pharaoh to let Moses and the people leave. Moses then led the people into the Sinai Peninsula.

The last forty years of Moses' life were spent in this wilderness. God gave Moses the Ten Commandments here (Exodus 20:1–24). Moses built the tabernacle, following God's instructions (Exodus 35–40). At one point, when the Israelites were without water in Kadesh, they grumbled and God told Moses to speak to a large rock to cause water to come from it. Moses, frustrated with the people, hit the rock with his staff. Though water still gushed from the rock (Numbers 20:2–11), God was angry with Moses' disobedience and their failure to honor God in front of the others. So God said Moses and Aaron would not be the ones to lead His people into the Promised Land (Numbers 20:12). God let Moses view the Promised Land from Mount Nebo, where he died at age 120 (Deuteronomy 34:1–7).

131. Mount Ararat

The place where Noah's ark landed (Genesis 8:4). **Mount Ararat is in modern-day Turkey, and rises higher than any other mountain in its range. Ancient Persians called Ararat "Noah's mountain," though no one knows the exact spot where the ark landed. Some people have searched for its remains on Mount Urartu in eastern Armenia.

132. Mount of Olives

A hill beyond the Kidron Valley east of Jerusalem. Many stories in the Bible took place at the Mount of Olives. Jesus often went to the Mount of Olives (Luke 22:39), and had an important talk with His disciples there (Matthew 24:3–26:2). This is where Judas betrayed Jesus the night before He was crucified (Matthew 26:30, 47). It's also where Jesus talked to the disciples after He rose from the dead (Acts 1:1–12). In Old Testament times, the branches of olive trees from this place were used to make booths for a special feast (Nehemiah 8:15).

133. NAZARETH

JESUS' BOYHOOD HOMETOWN. Nazareth is a village in Galilee near the Plain of Esdraelon. Mount Carmel is fifteen miles to the northwest. Nazareth is where Mary was when the angel told her she was going to give birth to Jesus (Luke 1:26–38). Mary, Joseph, and Jesus came back here after they had run away to Egypt (Matthew 2:20–23). Nazareth was where Jesus lived as a boy, gaining the name "Jesus of Nazareth" (Mark 1:24). The people of Nazareth were often offended by things Jesus said, and one time they tried to throw Him off a cliff (Luke 4:16–30)!

134. NEBUCHADNEZZAR

A POWERFUL KING OF BABYLONIA. Nebuchadnezzar's father began the Chaldean Empire, and Nebuchadnezzar was in charge of his army. Nebuchadnezzar became king upon his father's death. As king, Nebuchadnezzar attacked Jerusalem and his soldiers took things made of gold, silver, and bronze from the temple. They burned the temple and took many people of Judah into exile. God allowed the devastation as punishment for Judah's sins (2 Chronicles 36:15–20).

135. New Covenant

God's final promise or agreement with His people. The prophet Jeremiah predicted this new agreement (Jeremiah 31:31–34), and Jesus' Passover meal with His disciples was a symbol of it. Jesus called the cup the "new covenant in my blood" (Luke 22:20 NIV). Christ is the one who makes this new and better agreement possible. "Christ died to rescue those who had sinned and broken the old agreement. Now he brings his chosen ones a new agreement with its guarantee of God's eternal blessings!" (Hebrews 9:15 CEV).

136. Nicodemus

A Pharisee who knew Jesus was the Messiah. Nicodemus talked with Jesus about the new birth, when Jesus told him a person must be saved—born of the Spirit—before he or she can get into God's kingdom (John 3:1–7). Nicodemus bravely warned the Jewish leaders not to judge Jesus before hearing what He had to say (John 7:50–51). Later, Nicodemus helped prepare Jesus' body for burial (John 19:39–42).

137. NOAH

THE ARK BUILDER. Noah was chosen by God to save life on earth by building a huge wooden boat to escape the great flood. Noah was the son of Lamech and the father of Shem, Ham, and Japheth. After he built the ark, the six-hundred-year-old Noah went inside with his family and each type of animal (Genesis 7:6–9). Then God sent rain that lasted forty days and nights—coupled with the "fountains of the great deep" (Genesis 7:11), water flooded the entire earth. When the flood ended, Noah's family and the animals left the ark. Noah built an altar to worship God (Genesis 8:20), and the Lord made a covenant, or promise, with Noah (Genesis 9:1–17), saying He would never again punish the entire earth by water. Noah died at the age of 950 (Genesis 9:29).

138. OMNIPOTENCE

GOD'S GREAT POWER. There are no limits to God's power. He controls nature (Amos 4:13). He also controls what happens to all nations (Amos 1–2).

139. OMNIPRESENCE

GOD'S GREAT PRESENCE. God is in all places at all times. No one can hide from Him (Jeremiah 23:23–24). God's Spirit is with us in all we do (John 14:3, 18).

140. OMNISCIENCE

GOD'S GREAT KNOWLEDGE. God is very wise and He knows all. Christ is the key to understanding all of God's wisdom and knowledge (Colossians 2:2–3).

141. PALESTINE

THE HOLY LAND. The name *Palestine* came from a Greek word that means "land of the Philistines." The giant warrior Goliath, felled by David, was a Philistine. Three great world religions came out of Palestine: Judaism, Christianity, and Islam.

142. PARABLE

A STORY THAT TEACHES A LESSON. A parable is like a fable, using comparisons to teach deep truths. Jesus often spoke in parables—His followers could understand them, but unbelievers could not. Examples of parables include:

The Wise and
    Foolish Builders . . . . Matthew 7:24–27
The Lost Sheep . . . . Luke 15:3–7
The Prodigal Son . . . . Luke 15:11–32
The Sower . . . . Matthew 13:3–23

143. PASSOVER

AN IMPORTANT JEWISH HOLIDAY. Passover is when Jews remember the Israelites' Exodus from Egypt. The Israelites were slaves in Egypt for many years, until God sent plagues on the country to convince the Pharaoh to let the people go. The last plague was the death of the firstborn of every Egyptian family. To protect the Israelites from this plague, God told His people to paint the blood of a lamb over the doors of their houses. When He came to take the firstborn, He would "pass over" the homes that had blood over the doors (Exodus 12:13). After all the Egyptian firstborn died, Pharaoh let the Israelites go.

144. PAUL

A JESUS-HATER WHO BECAME A CHRISTIAN MISSIONARY. At first, Paul (then known as Saul) was against Christianity. In fact, he wanted to arrest and kill those who taught about Jesus (Acts 9:1). One day, on the road to Damascus, a bright light shone around Saul from heaven. He fell to the ground and heard Jesus' voice: "Saul, Saul, why do you persecute me?" (Acts 9:4 NIV). Jesus told Saul—who had been blinded by the light—to get up and go to Damascus. Saul was without his sight for three days. Then God sent a man named Ananias to heal Saul's eyes. Saul became a strong believer in Jesus, and was soon known as Paul. He took long missionary trips to share the Gospel, and wrote many of the books in the New Testament.

145. Pentecost

THE DAY ON WHICH THE HOLY SPIRIT WAS GIVEN TO BELIEVERS. *Pentecost* comes from the Greek word *pentekoste*, which means "fiftieth." In the Old Testament, Pentecost was a harvest festival (the Feast of Harvest, Exodus 23:16), celebrated fifty days after the Passover lamb was killed. In New Testament times, Pentecost was the day when the Holy Spirit came to earth to live in Jesus' followers (Acts 2:1–42). That happened fifty days after Jesus—known as *the Lamb of God*—was killed. When the Holy Spirit came, believers were filled with great joy, and Jesus' disciples worked many miracles. The church grew rapidly.

146. Persecution

OPPRESSION FOR ONE'S BELIEFS. Jesus was persecuted because He said He was the Son of God. His followers were persecuted for believing in Him. Jesus said that when believers are persecuted, God will bless them (Matthew 5:10). He also taught that we should pray for people who persecute us (Matthew 5:44). Faith in God helps us to handle persecution (Ephesians 6:16).

147. PERSIA

A GREAT NATION OF OLD TESTAMENT TIMES. Persia was a country covering most of the same territory as modern-day Iran. The Persians conquered Babylon in 539 BC. Then they began to allow the Israelites to leave their captivity (2 Chronicles 36:20–23). The Persian king Artaxerxes let Nehemiah go back to Jerusalem to rebuild the city wall (Nehemiah 2:1–8). Alexander the Great defeated the Persians around 330 BC.

148. PETER

ONE OF JESUS' CLOSEST FRIENDS. Also known as Simon, Peter was one of Jesus' twelve disciples, called away from his job as a fisherman. Peter was daring and impetuous, the disciple who cut off a man's ear when he came to arrest Jesus (John 18:10). Jesus scolded Peter and healed the man. When Peter saw Jesus walking on water, he asked to join Jesus and walked on the water—briefly—as well (Matthew 14:25–32). Before Jesus was arrested, Peter promised that he would be forever loyal; but when Jesus was taken away, Peter denied that he'd ever known Him. In the end, Jesus forgave Peter, and Peter did stay true to his Lord. Peter was one of the first two disciples to discover that Jesus had risen from the dead (John 20:1–10).

149. PHARISEES

A POWERFUL GROUP OF JEWISH LEADERS. In Jesus' time, the Pharisees were somewhat like a political party, concerned with the laws of the land. The Pharisees stayed true to the oldest laws and traditions of Israel. But Jesus disagreed with their perspective, emphasizing rules over more important things, like justice, mercy, and love. (See Matthew 23:1–7.) The Pharisees picked apart Jesus' words and actions, accusing Him of breaking the law. For example, the Pharisees were very unhappy when Jesus "worked" by healing a man on the Sabbath (Luke 6:6–11).

150. PHILIP

A NAME SHARED BY ONE OF THE DISCIPLES AND AN EARLY CHURCH LEADER. Jesus invited the first Philip to follow Him, and Philip brought along a friend named Nathanael (John 1:43–51). Both men became Jesus' disciples. This Philip once brought a group of Gentiles to see Jesus when He was in Jerusalem (John 12:20–22). The other Philip was chosen to help the twelve apostles in the church at Jerusalem (Acts 6:1–7). He was said to be honest, wise, and "full of the Holy Ghost" (Acts 6:3).

151. Pilate, Pontius

A ROMAN GOVERNOR OF JUDEA. Pilate supervised Jesus' trial, though he didn't want to be responsible for Jesus' crucifixion (John 18:28–38). At one point, Pilate sent Jesus to another ruler, Herod, for sentencing. But Herod sent Him back to Pilate (Luke 23:11). The trial took place at Passover time, and each year at Passover, a criminal was set free. Pilate suggested Jesus be released, but the jealous religious leaders stirred the people to call for a prisoner named Barabbas. Pilate ultimately turned Jesus over to be killed, but tried to avoid responsibility by symbolically washing his hands of the case (Matthew 27:24).

152. Pillar of Fire and Cloud

SIGNS OF GOD'S PRESENCE FOR THE ISRAELITES. When the people were traveling in the wilderness, God gave them signs that He was with them (Numbers 14:13–14). In the daytime, He was in a giant cloud to guide the people on their way. At night, He was in a tall pillar of fire (Exodus 13:21).

153. PLAGUE

A DISASTER. God sent ten plagues on Egypt because its leader wouldn't let the Israelites under Moses leave the country (Exodus 7–11). The plagues were:

1. Water turned into blood (Exodus 7:14–25)
2. Frogs everywhere (Exodus 8:1–15)
3. Lice on everything (Exodus 8:16–19)
4. Swarms of flies (Exodus 8:20–32)
5. Disease on farm animals (Exodus 9:1–7)
6. Boils and sores on humans (Exodus 9:8–12)
7. Destructive hail (Exodus 9:13–35)
8. Swarms of locusts (Exodus 10:1–20)
9. Utter darkness for three days
   (Exodus 10:21–29)
10. Death of firstborn children
    (Exodus 11:1–12:36)

The first nine plagues weren't enough to convince the Egyptian pharaoh to let the Israelites go. But when his own son died in the tenth plague, he urged Moses and the people to leave.

154. PRAYER

TALKING TO GOD. God is so powerful that He can talk—and listen—to everyone at once. In prayer, we can ask God to help us and others (Ephesians 6:18). We can request the things we need (Luke 11:3). We can tell God that we're sorry for our sins (1 John 1:9). We can even pray to God when we just need someone to talk to. After we talk to God, we can take time to listen for what He might be saying to us.

155. PRODIGAL SON

THE MAIN CHARACTER IN ONE OF JESUS' PARABLES. Jesus told the story of a young man whose father gave him a lot of money. The young man took the money and went off in search of pleasure. He spent the money foolishly until there was nothing left. By then, he was poor and starving. Not knowing what else to do, the man decided to go home to apologize and offer himself as a servant to his father. But when the older man saw him coming, he was filled with joy. The father put on a huge welcome-home party, picturing God the Father's pleasure when sinful people come to Him. Read more in Luke 15:11–32.

156. Publican

A TAX COLLECTOR. Tax collectors collected money for the Roman government. Matthew was a publican (Matthew 9:9–11). So was Zacchaeus (Luke 19:1–10).

157. Rabbi

A TITLE OF RESPECT MEANING "MASTER" OR "TEACHER." Mary Magdalene called Jesus "Rabboni" when He appeared to her after rising from His tomb (John 20:16). *Rabboni* is the Aramaic form of *Rabbi*. Nicodemus also used this name for Jesus, saying, "Rabbi, we know that you are a teacher who has come from God" (John 3:2 NIV). The disciples of Jesus called Him "Rabbi," too (John 1:38). This title was also used for John the Baptist by his followers (John 3:26). This word is still used in the Jewish faith today for leaders of the congregation and those who teach Jewish law.

158. Rainbow

AN ARCH OF COLORS IN THE SKY. A rainbow appeared after the great flood, a sign from God that He would never destroy the earth with water again (Genesis 9:9–17).

159. Rapture, the

A CONCEPT OF CHRIST'S RETURN TO EARTH. Many believe that when Jesus comes back, the redeemed will be changed, gaining glorified bodies like Christ's (Philippians 3:20–21) as they're taken up into the clouds to meet the Lord. The "dead in Christ" will also be raised at that time (1 Thessalonians 4:16–17).

160. Red Sea

A BODY OF WATER BETWEEN EGYPT AND ARABIA. God split the Red Sea in two when Moses led the Israelites out of Egypt. God told Moses to hold his walking stick over the sea and a miracle occurred—the people of Israel walked across the sea on dry land, with water on both sides. The Egyptian army, pursuing the Israelites, went into the middle of the water; but the sea came back together, drowning every soldier. Read more in Exodus 14.

161. RESURRECTION

RISING FROM THE DEAD. For believers, resurrection leads to eternal life. Jesus taught His followers to believe in the resurrection, saying, "My Father wants everyone who sees the Son to have faith in him and to have eternal life. Then I will raise them to life on the last day" (John 6:40 CEV). Paul also taught that Jesus would give Christians life that lasts forever (Romans 2:7)—and Jesus provided proof when He Himself rose to life after the crucifixion.

162. RUTH

A WOMAN OF GREAT LOYALTY. The brief Old Testament book of Ruth tells her story. She was from Moab, but married a son of the Israelite Naomi. Later, Naomi's husband and both sons died. Naomi wanted to go home to Judea, and loyal Ruth moved with her to Bethlehem (Ruth 1:16–19). There, Ruth worked in the fields owned by a man named Boaz. He was related to Naomi, and ultimately married Ruth. Their descendants included King David and ultimately Jesus (Ruth 4:9–22; Matthew 1:1–6).

163. SABBATH

SATURDAY, THE SEVENTH DAY OF THE WEEK. The Sabbath is the Jewish day of worship, a symbol of the day God rested after His creation (Genesis 2:2). Most Christians worship on the first day of the week—Sunday. Sunday (1 Corinthians 16:2) is the day Jesus rose from the dead. One of the Ten Commandments says that the Sabbath is a special day that should be kept holy (Exodus 20:8). Jesus was criticized for not keeping the Old Testament Sabbath rules (Matthew 12:1–14). He responded by saying the Sabbath was made for man, not man for the Sabbath (Mark 2:27).

164. SALT

A SEASONING. Salt is a mineral used to season and preserve food. Jesus called His followers "the salt of the earth" (Matthew 5:13), meaning they should flavor and benefit the world around them. Jesus warned about Christians losing their saltiness (Luke 14:34). If salt loses its flavor, it isn't good for anything—and if a believer loses his purity, neither is he.

165. SALVATION

GOD'S WORK OF DELIVERING HUMANS FROM SIN. **Salvation is** available to everyone, but it's only possible by believing in Jesus Christ (Romans 8:9; Hebrews 5:9). Jesus' death made it possible for anyone to live in heaven with God someday (John 3:36). This salvation protects us from the punishment of hell: "For God hath not appointed us to wrath, but to obtain salvation by our Lord Jesus Christ" (1 Thessalonians 5:9 KJV).

166. SAMARIA

IN BIBLE TIMES, BOTH A REGION AND A CITY. **Samaria was the** main city of the northern kingdom of Israel. Omri, a king of Israel, built the city in about 900 BC. Samaria was also the name of the whole area around that city. The Assyrians took over Samaria (2 Kings 17:24) around 722 BC, and mixed the Jewish people there with other cultures. The "Samaritans," as the mixed people were called, were hated by the Jews. Jesus, however, showed compassion for Samaritans, healing a man of leprosy in Samaria (Luke 17:11–19) and talking with a Samaritan woman at a well (John 4:1–30). Today, Samaria is part of an area called the West Bank.

167. SAMUEL

THE LAST JUDGE OF ISRAEL (1 SAMUEL 7:15–17). Samuel was also a prophet (1 Samuel 3:19–20). As a little boy, he was taken to the tabernacle to learn from a priest named Eli (1 Samuel 1:23–2:11). As a man, he became the Israelites' leader. Samuel led the people in worshipping God, and oversaw a long period of peace. When Samuel was old, he anointed Saul as Israel's first king (1 Samuel 10:20–24). After Saul disobeyed God, Samuel anointed David the new king (1 Samuel 16:13). Upon Samuel's death, he was given a huge funeral: "People from all over Israel gathered to mourn for him" (1 Samuel 25:1 CEV).

168. SARAH

ABRAHAM'S WIFE (GENESIS 11:29) AND MOTHER OF ISAAC. Sarah was also called *Sarai*. She was more than ninety years old when Isaac was born. Her husband was one hundred years old (Genesis 17:17)! God said that He would bless Sarah, that she would become "a mother of nations" (Genesis 17:16). She was an ancestor to all the Israelites, kings, and even to Jesus. Sarah was 127 years old when she died. Her supposed burial site, called the Tomb of the Patriarchs, is a popular tourist site near Hebron, about twenty miles from Jerusalem.

169. SATAN

ANOTHER NAME FOR THE DEVIL. Jesus called Satan "the father of lies" (John 8:44). His work goes as far back as the Garden of Eden, where, as a serpent, he tempted Eve to eat the forbidden fruit (Genesis 3:1–6). Jesus also called Satan "the prince of this world" (John 16:11), but his power is limited to what God allows him. In the end, Satan will be cast into the lake of fire forever (Revelation 20:10).

170. SEA OF GALILEE

A LAKE IN THE NORTHERN PART OF ISRAEL. A freshwater lake about fourteen miles long and seven miles wide, the Sea of Galilee is a popular place for fishermen. Several of Jesus' disciples—James, John, Peter, and Andrew—fished there (Mark 1:16–20). Jesus spent a lot of time near this sea. Once, during a bad storm, He and his disciples were in a boat tossed by the waves. Jesus told the water to calm down, and it did (Matthew 8:23–27). Jesus also walked on water in the Sea of Galilee (John 6:16–20).

171. Second Coming

J ESUS' RETURN TO EARTH. Before Jesus ascended to heaven He
said He would come back—and without any warning. He
urged Christians to be prepared (Matthew 24:42). When Jesus
comes, He will raise the dead (1 Thessalonians 4:16) and take
believers with Him into the air. The Second Coming also starts
a chain of events that bring the end of life as we know it. Jesus
will punish wicked people who won't believe in Him.

172. Sennacherib

A N ASSYRIAN KING. He captured all the cities in Judah
except Jerusalem, but extracted tribute money from King
Hezekiah (2 Kings 18:13–16). King Sennacherib died as he
worshipped a false god (2 Kings 19:36–37). His own sons killed
him.

173. Sermon on the Mount

WIDE-RANGING TEACHINGS OF JESUS. Large crowds followed Jesus wherever He went, and one time He preached to them from a hillside near Capernaum. Jesus told the people how to find happiness (Matthew 5:3–12), encouraged them to speak up about God (Matthew 5:13–16), reminded them about God's commandments (Matthew 5:17–48), and said they should give to the needy (Matthew 6:1–4). Jesus taught them the Lord's Prayer (Matthew 6:9–13) and other rules about prayer and fasting (Matthew 6:14–18), and told them not to love money more than God (Matthew 6:19–24). He even told the people how to be free from worry (Matthew 6:25–34). Jesus ended His sermon with a parable about obeying God's Word (Matthew 7:24–27).

174. Shekinah

GOD'S VISIBLE GLORY. The Bible tells of God appearing in a cloud, fire, and a bright light. When the Israelites left Egypt, God led them in a cloud and a column of fire (Exodus 13:20–22). God talked to Moses through a burning bush (Exodus 3). On the night Jesus was born, the glory of God showed as a very bright light that frightened shepherds in the fields (Luke 2:9).

175. SHILOH

ISRAEL'S FIRST CAPITAL CITY. The tabernacle was located here, and inside the tabernacle, the ark of the covenant. Over time, the Israelites became careless with God. Once, in a battle with the Philistines, the Israelites took the ark from Shiloh onto the battlefield as a sort of good luck charm. It didn't work—the Philistines captured the ark (1 Samuel 4:3–11).

176. SIN

THE BAD THINGS THAT PEOPLE DO. Sin is disobedience toward God, which began with Adam and Eve in the Garden of Eden. From that point on, everyone has sinned (Romans 5:12–14). Sin is not only our behavior toward God; it's also how we treat others and ourselves. Nobody can be perfect before God, so He sent Jesus to die on the cross and take the punishment for our sins (Romans 5:8). Without Jesus, no one would be good enough to get into heaven (Romans 3:10).

177. SODOM AND GOMORRAH

WICKED CITIES IN THE TIME OF ABRAHAM (GENESIS 14:1–3). The people of Sodom and Gomorrah were perverse and violent. A righteous man named Lot was troubled by the behavior of his neighbors (2 Peter 2:7), and God sent two angels to warn him of the approaching destruction of the cities. Lot took his wife and two daughters by the hand and started running. An angel said, "Run for your lives! Don't even look back. And don't stop in the valley. Run to the hills, where you will be safe" (Genesis 19:17 CEV). But Lot's wife looked back and turned into a block of salt. Then God destroyed Sodom and Gomorrah with fire and brimstone (Genesis 19:23–29).

178. SOLOMON

A WISE KING, SON OF KING DAVID. Solomon followed David as
a king of Israel. When God offered the new king anything
he wished, Solomon prayed that God would give him wisdom
(1 Kings 3). He became famous for his wisdom and his wealth
(1 Kings 4:20–34); and at God's command, Solomon built a
temple at Jerusalem (1 Kings 5–8). Later, though, Solomon
drifted away from God after he married wives who worshipped
idols (1 Kings 11:1–8). Solomon put heavy taxes on his people
(1 Kings 12:4); and after he died, many rebelled against his son
Rehoboam and the nation was divided. The rebels formed the
northern kingdom of Israel, where Solomon's servant, Jeroboam,
ruled. Rehoboam ruled the southern kingdom of Judah. Read
more in 1 Kings 12:1–19.

179. SPIRITUAL GIFTS

SPECIAL ABILITIES GIVEN TO BELIEVERS. The Bible lists many gifts that God's Holy Spirit can give to believers. The greatest of these is love (1 Corinthians 13:13), while other gifts of the Spirit are preaching, serving, teaching, encouraging, giving, leading, and helping (Romans 12:6–8). Wisdom, knowledge, faith, and discernment are also His gifts (1 Corinthians 12:8–11).

180. STEPHEN

ONE OF THE FIRST DEACONS OF THE CHRISTIAN CHURCH (ACTS 6:5). Stephen was "a man full of faith and of the Holy Ghost" (Acts 6:5 KJV). His job as deacon was to help Jesus' twelve disciples, allowing them to teach and pray while Stephen and six other men served the physical needs of church members. But God also gave Stephen the gift of performing miracles (Acts 6:8). The Jewish leaders didn't like Stephen's influence with the people (Acts 6:10), and they had him arrested and stoned to death. As he was dying, Stephen said: "Lord Jesus, receive my spirit. . . . Do not hold this sin against them" (Acts 7:59–60 NIV).

181. STONING

AN ANCIENT PUNISHMENT. When a person was stoned, others stood around and threw rocks at that person until he or she died. Godly men were sometimes stoned because of their faith. Stephen was one of them (Acts 7:59).

182. SYNAGOGUE

A JEWISH CHURCH BUILDING. Paul taught about Jesus in synagogues during his missionary journeys (Acts 18:4).

183. TABERNACLE

APORTABLE WORSHIP CENTER. In early Israel, there was no permanent worship center. The tabernacle was a large tent where people worshipped. God told the Israelites to build His tabernacle in the wilderness, calling it the "tent of meeting" (Exodus 40:1–8 NIV). It was specially made to be moved from place to place. Animals were sacrificed to God at the tabernacle (Leviticus 1:1–9), symbols of what was to come. The greatest sacrifice of all—Jesus' death on the cross—ended the need for animal sacrifice (Hebrews 7:27).

184. TEMPLE

ISRAEL'S PLACE OF WORSHIP. After the death of King David, the Jewish people worshipped at the temple in Jerusalem. Solomon built the first one, a beautiful structure ninety feet long, thirty feet wide, and forty-five feet high. It had a porch that was thirty feet long and fifteen feet wide (1 Kings 6:3). Some of its walls were covered with gold and decorated with precious stones. The ark of the covenant was kept in the temple. Read more about this temple in 2 Chronicles 3–4. After about 350 years, the Israelites' enemy, the Babylonians, destroyed Solomon's temple. A second temple was built about seventy years after that, under the direction of a man named Zerubbabel. Then a few years before Jesus was born, King Herod the Great began to build a bigger, more impressive temple on the same site. It was destroyed by the Roman army in AD 70.

185. TEMPTATION

AN INNER DRAW TOWARD SIN. Everyone has faced temptation, even Jesus. Read how Satan tempted Jesus in Matthew 4:1–11. The Lord's Prayer (Matthew 6:9–13) teaches us to ask God to protect us from temptation. The Bible says God will help us when we are tempted (1 Corinthians 10:13).

186. TEN COMMANDMENTS

AN IMPORTANT SEGMENT OF GOD'S LAW. God gave the Ten Commandments to Moses (Exodus 20:1–17), telling him to share them with the people of Israel. The Ten Commandments are:

1. Have no other gods before God (Exodus 20:3).
2. Don't worship idols (Exodus 20:4).
3. Don't use God's name in a disrespectful way (Exodus 20:7).
4. Keep the Sabbath as a day to honor God (Exodus 20:8).
5. Respect your parents (Exodus 20:12).
6. Don't murder (Exodus 20:13).
7. Don't commit adultery (Exodus 20:14).
8. Don't steal (Exodus 20:15).
9. Don't lie (Exodus 20:16).
10. Don't covet—that is, desire things that belong to others (Exodus 20:17).

187. THOMAS

THE DOUBTING DISCIPLE. He was also called *Didymus*, which means "twin" (John 11:16). Thomas was one of Jesus' original twelve disciples (Matthew 10:2–4), best known for doubting the resurrection of Christ. Thomas demanded proof, saying he wanted to see the nail marks on Jesus' hands and the hole in His side where He'd been stuck with a spear. So Jesus showed him, and Thomas believed. Jesus told Thomas that he had believed what he could see. But there is a special blessing for people who believe God without seeing proof. Read more in John 20:24–29.

188. TIMOTHY

PAUL'S YOUNG FRIEND, CALLED "MY SON IN THE FAITH" (1 TIMOTHY 1:2). Timothy's father was Greek, and his mother Jewish. He was raised as a Christian by his mother, Eunice, and grandmother, Lois, both women of strong faith (2 Timothy 1:5). Paul and Timothy traveled together and taught others about Jesus, sharing imprisonment in Rome for a while (Hebrews 13:23). Later, Paul wrote two letters to the young man, the New Testament books called 1 and 2 Timothy.

189. TOWER OF BABEL

THE BIRTHPLACE OF MULTIPLE LANGUAGES. Not long after the flood, humans banded together to build a tall tower and make a name for themselves. God upset their prideful plans by giving the people different languages so they couldn't understand one another, then scattered them around the world. The name Babel comes from the Hebrew word for "confuse." Read more in Genesis 11:1–9.

190. TRANSFIGURATION

A CHANGING. Jesus once took Peter, James, and John up a high mountain where Jesus' appearance changed. His face glowed like the sun and His clothes became like a bright, white light. This "transfiguration" frightened the disciples, who were surprised to see the Old Testament figures Moses and Elijah appear with Jesus. Then God's voice boomed from a cloud, saying, "This is my beloved Son, in whom I am well pleased; hear ye him" (Matthew 17:5 KJV).

191. TRINITY, THE

GOD THE FATHER, JESUS THE SON, AND THE HOLY SPIRIT. *Trinity* means "three." The "Godhead" (Colossians 2:9 KJV) is three persons in one:

1) God, our heavenly Father (Ephesians 3:14–15);
2) Jesus, the Son of God (John 11:27), on earth as God in the
   form of man; and
3) the Holy Spirit, who convicts (John 16:8) and guides (John 1
   6:13–15) people, giving believers special talents and
   encouraging them to use those "gifts" for God.

192. TWELVE, THE

JESUS' ORIGINAL DISCIPLES. These were the men Jesus chose personally (John 15:16) to travel with Him and help Him teach. The twelve were Peter, Andrew, James the son of Zebedee, John, Philip, Bartholomew, Thomas, Matthew, James the son of Alphaeus, Thaddaeus, Simon, and Judas Iscariot (Matthew 10:2–4). Jesus allowed the twelve to cast out evil spirits and heal sick people (Matthew 10:1). Most of them apparently suffered martyrdom after the New Testament was written.

193. Unleavened Bread

BREAD MADE WITHOUT YEAST. Without yeast, bread dough doesn't rise. This "unleavened" bread is flat, and the subject of a Jewish festival. The Feast of the Unleavened Bread celebrates the Israelites' escape from Egypt (Exodus 13:3), recalling how quickly the escaping slaves left the country. The Israelites departed in such a hurry that they had no time to put yeast into their bread mix. Instead, they wrapped the dough in cloth and rushed away (Exodus 12:33–34).

194. Urim and Thummim

PRIESTLY OBJECTS FROM OLD TESTAMENT TIMES. The exact nature of the Urim and Thummim is a mystery, but they might have been colored stones or metal. These objects were in the breastplate of the high priest Aaron (Exodus 28:30). They may have been cast as lots to show the will of God (Numbers 27:21).

195. VIRGIN BIRTH

HOW JESUS CAME INTO THIS WORLD. An angel visited Jesus' mother, Mary, telling her that she would have a very special baby named Jesus (Luke 1:31–33). But Mary asked, "How will this be, since I am a virgin?" (Luke 1:34 NIV). The angel answered, "The Holy Spirit will come on you, and the power of the Most High will overshadow you. So the holy one to be born will be called the Son of God" (Luke 1:35 NIV). Being the Son of God made Jesus holy. But being born to a human mother made Him like His own creation. *Immanuel* is a Hebrew word that means "God is with us." Long before Jesus was born, the prophet Isaiah predicted this amazing birth, saying, "The Lord himself will give you a sign: The virgin will conceive and give birth to a son, and will call him Immanuel" (Isaiah 7:14 NIV).

196. WITNESS

A PERSON TELLS WHAT HE OR SHE KNOWS. A witness gives "testimony," just like in a court of law. In Bible times, the testimony of at least two witnesses was needed to find a person guilty of a capital crime (Deuteronomy 17:6). Anyone who told lies while testifying was punished (Deuteronomy 19:18–19). As New Testament believers, we are called to be witnesses for Christ (Acts 1:8).

197. WORSHIP

PRAISING AND ADORING GOD. Worship can occur at church, but God can be worshipped anywhere (Deuteronomy 6:5–7). A person can worship God alone or with others (Daniel 6:10; Psalm 132:7). In Bible times, the Jews worshipped in the tabernacle until they started using the temple. After they were taken to live among the Babylonians and Persians, they worshipped in synagogues. The book of Psalms, essentially the Jewish hymn book, is full of praise and worship for God. Psalm 95:6 says, "Bow down and worship the LORD our Creator!" (CEV).

198. YAHWEH

A KEY OLD TESTAMENT NAME FOR GOD. In Hebrew, Yahweh appears as these four letters: Read the letters from right to left. In English, it looks like the four consonants YHWH. Many Bibles today translate the word *Yahweh* as Lord or Jehovah.

199. ZACCHAEUS

A SHORT TAX COLLECTOR. One day, as Jesus passed through Jericho, crowds came out to see Him. Since Zacchaeus was "little of stature" (Luke 19:3 KJV), he climbed a tree to get a better look at Jesus. When Jesus saw Zacchaeus in the tree, He told him to come down, "for to day I must abide at thy house" (Luke 19:5 KJV). Zacchaeus hurried to Jesus and promised to make amends for any cheating he'd done as a tax collector. Zacchaeus said he would give half of his money to the poor and pay back anyone he had cheated, fourfold. Jesus was pleased with Zacchaeus's choice, saying, "This day is salvation come to this house" (Luke 19:9 KJV).

If you enjoyed

THE BIBLE BRIEF

be sure to look for these other great Bible
resources from Barbour Publishing!

The Complete Guide to the Bible
Paperback, 528 pages
ISBN 978-1-59789-374-9

500 Questions & Answers
from the Bible
Paperback, 256 pages
ISBN 978-1-59789-473-9

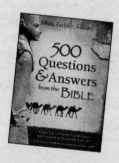

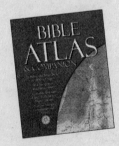

Bible Atlas & Companion
Paperback, 176 pages
ISBN 978-1-59789-779-2

Available wherever Christian books are sold.